LOVE CONQUERS ALL?

ONE WOMAN'S STORY

You're not alone

Introduction

Remember, sometimes the best choices are the hardest ones to make!

I wonder, if a man could see the devastation to the one he says he loves, would he make the same choices?

There are so many different scenarios of cheating and thankfully I have not experienced them all, but those I have experienced have had such a devastating effect on who I am that I really don't know if you ever fully recover.

So many people think that if there is no sex involved it is not cheating; well tell that to the heart because from my experience the heart isn't quite sure there is a difference.

I am not a professional therapist or counselor and I do not have a degree from some special school. I am just me, a wife, a mother, a daughter, an aunt and a friend and most of all, a woman.

I know that when I was going through some of the toughest times in my life, I had never felt so alone. Oh I had friends that were always there for me, but if you have ever experienced infidelity you will know what I mean when I say you can be in a room full of people and feel like you are the only one in the world.

It is a hurt that has many faces. I never knew that so many emotions could exist let alone that you could feel so many of them all at the same time. I was the one that was let down, betrayed and damaged. I remember feeling how very unfair. Here he gets to go out and have his fun, experience whatever temptation it was that was so impossible to say no to, the one that made it worth risking everything we had built together, and yet here I was the only one with the hurdles to cross and the heartache to repair not to mention trust, intimacy, friendship, self-worth, confidence and forgiveness to find.

I know that while my world was falling apart I could have used the words of someone who had been there. Not a fix, not a self-help book just the words of someone that had been through the same heartache that would understand. Maybe had I been able to read their story I wouldn't have felt quite so alone or went down the road I did.

How many of you out there have heard the words "forget it and move on", "quit dwelling on it", "why are you doing this to yourself", "don't obsess"? Well I have heard each and every one. Why is it that no one seems to understand none of the above are a choice? These are not feelings that are fun to feel or emotions we seek out for what, self-pleasure? Do people not understand that we would gladly never experience another memory of the man we love with some woman if only, it was a choice?

Men are looking for forgiveness and they get angry when it isn't given quite fast enough, but ladies tell me this, how many men would still be even considering a future with us if the tables were turned? I was to find out. This is a concept that never seems to enter their minds when they make that mistake that changes everything and they all seem to hide behind the same excuse, we're men we can't help it, men are testosterone driven, we weren't made to be monogamous. Please save it, do they not think women have a sex drive, a need to feel sexy, a need to feel desired, a want for the feeling of new, the excitement of taboo? I am not saying women never cheat, I'm just saying in my experience these are all excuses for bad choices and self-absorbed behaviour.

So I am telling you my story, maybe as much to help me as to help you. I'm not looking for sympathy or answers because there aren't any no matter how many books you read about forgiveness and how if you turn the other cheek love will get you through. No one will get you through but you. It is a choice to move forward and each person must decide whether to stay or to go. Some people say it is easier to just leave and move on. I chose to stay. It hasn't been an easy choice but one I hope in the long run is worth the effort.

Hence, I am left with the old saying of "once a cheater always a cheater" and wondering if in time I will find that it is true or if men can really change.

Here is my story!

Chapter One

The Beginning

Every heartache begins with a love story. Mine is no exception.

I had a lot of lessons to learn and a lot of growing up to do. As you read my story, I hope you understand that love was never the issue between Mark and me. We had a lot of hurdles to overcome and it certainly wasn't an easy road but one when you finish taking the journey with me, I think you will understand, nothing is black and white. So, the beginning:

As I look back to that very first moment I saw my future, I still smile even after everything we have been through. There is still that moment in time when all seemed right with the world.

I was a young woman newly separated with two small children, three and five. I had never really been single and after seven years of marriage I realized I had married my best friend. The only problem with marrying your best friend is there is no passion. I guess I wanted to experience dating and see what life was going on outside my little family.

I don't regret marrying my high school sweetheart as it is because of him that I was blessed with the two greatest gifts in my life, my two sons. However, I also knew that I had to leave the marriage if we were both to find out who we were outside of adolescence.

When I met Mark I wasn't looking for a life partner, far from it and I really didn't think I was attracted to him at all but, I did find myself seeking out his company for what reason I had yet to figure out. We just didn't seem able to stay away from each other. He was only a year and a half out of his first marriage to his high school sweetheart as well and was still mending a broken heart.

I really believe in my soul that Mark is a good man and I think he was given a really bad start in life and he was raised with a very bad belief system. Mark grew up always hearing from his mother how men cheat, men can't be trusted, all men fail. This is so sad. I do remember so much good about Mark, there must have been some right? Otherwise, what did I fall so madly in love with and madly in love I certainly did fall.

Our romance was fast to flourish and seemed to take on a life of its own in no time. He was affectionate and I loved that part of him. He was always holding my hand in public and whenever we would stand talking to friends he would always stand me in front of him with his arms around my waist to keep me close. Kisses were abundant. I was completely and totally in love with this man. The one thing that is so dear to my heart is the way he would slow dance with me. He has this way of wiggling his hips when he dances, and when he held me close everyone else in the room disappeared and I was alone with just him. It always used to amaze me how he could so easily make this happen.

We moved in together after only four months of dating and no decision in my life ever felt so right to me. I think for Mark it wasn't quite so clear. He was so good to my children and to me but right from the beginning there was a part of him that he held back from me. I think maybe it had something to do with his childhood and the abuse he grew up in.

He was told from a very young age that he wasn't wanted and he was never let to forget this fact while growing up. His father left before he was born and his mother never failed to inform him that it was his fault that his father left. He grew up with his mother and a sister. He left home at an early age and struggled to finish high school and to support himself working nights.

He fell in love with a young girl who stole his heart even though he tried to run. He married her directly out of high school. It wasn't long until he realized that her heart wasn't in the relationship to the extent that his was and repeatedly she left him for one reason or another. Again he learned the lesson that he wasn't good enough and love couldn't be trusted and it certainly didn't last. He took the risk to give his heart to this young girl only to have it broken more than once.

When his marriage ended he had a broken heart as it was her that didn't want the marriage and he was left with no choice, a broken heart and a lot of debt. It was instilled even deeper in his heart that women couldn't be trusted especially with your heart and he made the decision to never get married again and to never let a woman that close again. I think it was at this point that he started to believe it was safer to make the woman always feel you had one foot out the door. It kept them pursuing him. It was a year and a half later that he met me. It was on our first trip to Montreal in his transport, as he was a truck driver that I remember him telling me he would never get married again and he thought it important that I know that.

I remember the first night that he told me that he was falling in love with me and I don't think up until that moment I had ever been happier. He gave me as much as he was able to give at that point. I remember running to the women's bathroom with a girlfriend and I was ecstatic with joy and couldn't wait to share the news with her. When I told her she said "be careful. Mark has a reputation of treating women really well for a while and then he breaks their heart. Don't let him break your heart." I remember being rather upset at her words, here I was so happy he loved me and she just couldn't be happy for me. Still it didn't dampen my mood of pure joy.

I had never experienced heartache before. I guess I was one of the lucky ones. I jumped into this relationship from day one with all of me and no caution or reserve. I guess I started to see little signs right from the beginning that Mark had a problem with fidelity and not playing with any female within his vicinity. I think it was always safer for him to live life with one foot out the door, he always seemed to be preparing himself for the worst. At this point I thought he was only a big flirt and that I could keep him focused.

Mark and I did so much together. Every day seemed to be filled with a new adventure and just so much happiness for me. I was in love and I felt great.

I remember the simplest things made me so happy. There was a night that I was visiting Mark at his apartment and it was one of those nights you know just before a huge rain storm when you can feel the electricity in the air and there is that wind. Well we went for a walk. Me in my bathing suit top and shorts and Mark in a t-shirt and cut offs. Well we didn't get too far and it started to rain. Mark had his cigarettes with him and he didn't want them to get wet so we stopped in at the local sub shop and asked the man behind the counter to hold them for him, he would be back. We live in a small town where everyone knows everyone. Then the downpour started. I remember it was cold when the rain first hit your skin but once we were soaked the rain was so warm. Mark took me over to the side of a building and he held me under the downspout and the warm water just poured all over me. I felt like we were two kids out playing in the rain and splashing in the puddles. We ran and we laughed and we kissed and hugged. It was such a simple night yet one that will remain a cherished memory for me forever.

Mark was always able to make me laugh. I had never met anyone that could talk as much as Mark managed to talk. I found it very entertaining that he could start a conversation and during that initial conversation he would go off in about five different directions and the part that I found amazing was that by the time he was finished, he had concluded each and every one. He always had something funny to say.

As we all know infatuation and bliss can't last forever. No relationship will stand the test of time without some obstacles to cross. I guess it takes time to figure out if you have that kind of love and that kind of relationship. It is always a bit of a fall when the infatuation starts to wear off and you realize you love this person but you also realize just like everyone else your love to will take work at times.

My first experience with figuring out that Mark was a ladies man, as small as it is since we weren't really serious yet, was at a party we went to. We had a great time and it was a group of friends that Mark had previously hung out with and they were all new to me. When it came time to leave I headed to the car only to discover I had left my coat upstairs. I went back to the party, one to get my coat and the other to get my date. Mark is very social and he loves to talk more than most. When I walked into the party I opened the door only to look across the room and see Mark taking the glasses off of a girls' face only to bend down and kiss her. I just stared and he looked up at me with a smile on his face. I walked out of the party and headed for the car. I was hurt inside. I knew I had no right to demand he be exclusive but I really thought in my head he was as interested in me as I was in him and at least would respect that at least that night he hadn't come alone, he had brought a date, me. I remember we sat on the stairway of the apartment and talked, we joked about a lot of it and I remember saying to him "we need some ground rules right from the start here, nobody kisses nobody. You get that, nobody kisses nobody." He laughed and said "ok I get it. Nobody kisses nobody." We moved on.

Things progressed naturally and we had our circle of friends and went out quite often dancing and socializing. Most times at the bar I would find Mark talking to the female waitress or bartender or off socializing with a girl across the bar. He would go and dance with girls as well. I was always jealous and I didn't feel too great, being his date and being left behind while he wandered off on his own to socialize but I always pushed it down and convinced myself it was just Mark being social. He would even do this when we went shopping together. I would go look for clothes wanting him to give me his opinion when I tried them on but I always found him talking to the young cashier. Aside from his flirtatious nature, I thought life didn't get much better than this.

Chapter Two

My Introduction to Mark's Other Side

After about a year of living together little things were brought to my attention. I had a best friend, Trish, and we were inseparable. We did everything together. I knew Mark found her attractive everyone did. She was one of those girls that had everything in the right place and knew it and her confidence really attracted the men including mine. I thought, he knows she is my best friend so I don't ever have to worry about anything and I thought he was in love with me and he was the faithful type after having experienced his first wife's infidelity and knowing how it feels.

One day my friend came to me and said she had something to tell me that I wasn't going to like. She told me that Mark was making her very uncomfortable. She told me that when I left the room he went up to her and said "give me a hug". She said she didn't think much of it and she hugged him. The next time I left the room he again said "give me a hug and unbutton your shirt first". She thought he was joking around so she went and gave him a hug. After she hugged him he said to her "oh boobs that's something I'm not used to". I guess here is where I should tell you I was not well endowed that way but never really thought Mark cared about that. When she told me, I was very hurt and felt very inadequate in the physique department. I confronted Mark with what I was told and he simply said he was only joking. This was a phrase I would come to know very well.

As far as I know there was never anything else that happened between them but it did start to raise my awareness that maybe Mark just wasn't as into me as I was to him. I started to doubt myself at this point.

Mark was always the outspoken not shy, confident type and he will admit himself that sometimes he says things that hurt someone's feelings but he didn't mean it that way. Still the result is the same, hurt feelings. The one example I can give you of this is one day Trish and I were going to lay out on my back deck and sunbathe and we came walking through the kitchen in our bathing suits. I stopped to hug

Mark on my way through and he smiled and said "Hey, if you took the top half of her body and the bottom half of yours, you'd have the perfect body". I don't think he meant to hurt my feelings but as self-conscious as I was about being small busted, it did hurt and then I became very shy that way around Mark. I started to worry that if he really did find my small breasts not attractive and if he was always flirting with other women, how long would he stay with me. After all, my relationship with him was still very new. I started to think in the back of my mind that I would love to get breast implants. I had always been teased in high school for my flat chested physique but now that it was a source of anxiety in my relationship it really started to plague me. I must tell you Mark never complained seriously to me about having a problem with my physique so I think had I not had the demons in this regard from high school his comments wouldn't have run so deeply for me.

It was about this period of time when Mark developed some kind of illness. We were never given a diagnosis for the illness and to this day we are still searching. He started to experience pain in his testicle and after any sexual activity it would swell and understandably so his moods were not the best and his sex drive started to plummet. He seemed to be happy around everyone else and flirtatious with the girls as if nothing had changed in him but when we were alone together I saw the other side of him. I saw the distance, the anger and the withdrawal from me. Maybe I didn't understand enough or maybe I could have done more but this was a fairly new relationship and my only experience with love was one of the utmost friendship and honesty and mutual respect. This was new to me and I wasn't sure what to do with it. I started to believe his interest in me was diminishing and he was drifting away. I loved him terribly and tried to hang on tighter but he still was moving away from me and yet seemed happy when around others especially women. During this time Mark started to be very hurtful with the things he would say and he became so very distant with me. Our sex life which had always been so compatible and so amazing became a source of tension and hurt feelings. I really thought Mark no longer found me attractive and that was why he had the need to get the attention of every other girl in sight.

I don't know if all of the thoughts that I was experiencing were normal, really how can someone say what is normal and what is not. All I know is that the emotions that I was feeling, right or wrong, were very real to me and being my own there was nothing else for me to go on. I hope my honesty with all of you will at least if nothing else give some of you comfort if you have gone through a situation similar in your own life with the person you love. I really don't think I am the only one out there that loves so deeply and gets hurt so deeply and chooses to stay for love.

One night Mark and I went to the local dance bar and Mark's sister joined us for the evening. I remember Mark kept dancing with my friend Trish. He spent so much of the evening dancing with Trish that his sister pointed this out to me and she said "are you going to put up with that because I sure wouldn't". I didn't say anything to Mark that night but I did talk to him about it later and his response to me was "well Trish is fun to dance with, she moves around and you just stand there". Once again I felt so worthless. I have always found it so hard to get and to hold Mark's attention. Come to think of it, it wasn't long after he moved in with me that I started to feel like I was not good enough for him and I would never be good enough for him. He always seemed to need and want more.

Chapter Three

John

It was about this time that John, a friend
of Mark's started hanging around us a lot
and he had a girlfriend who was also a
friend of mine her name was Erin, so the
two of them were around quite often. Erin
was a very busty woman but not overly
attractive.   Mark still seemed very
attracted to her for some reason. Again,
maybe if he hadn't become ill and I didn't
feel him pulling away from me I wouldn't
have been so attentive in paying attention
to his interaction with other women.

There was a night that Erin came to a
friend's wedding with us and I will never
forget it because up to this point his
attraction to Erin was very subtle.   The
two of them got up to dance to the
Macarena and I have to admit she is a
great dancer. She was doing the moves to
the song but he was standing behind her
and she was in front of him with her back
to his front. He was laughing and joking
around and was doing the movements to
the dance as if he was doing them on her
and he held his hands out in front of her
breasts and then her hips etc. He didn't

touch her but they did wiggle together for the part of the song that has this movement. I was jealous of course, I knew he thought she was attractive for some reason and it was her he wanted to be dancing with not me. When he came back and sat down at our table in his dress pants, I noticed he was squirming and I went to put my hand on his upper thigh and he moved away. That made me very suspicious so I put my hand on him and noticed that he was erect. He had gotten turned on when he danced with her. I couldn't believe what that did to me. Their friendship was no longer innocent in my eyes.

From that moment on my self-image and desirability in my mind plummeted to an all-time low. I believed that he was attracted to yet another woman and his interest was not in me when we went out. My friendship with Erin started to change at that time and I didn't want her near Mark together alone but I knew there was nothing I could do to stop them. I really believed he no longer found me sexy and that his love for me was diminishing. It is so hard to describe what this does to you. I most times was quiet, felt sad and scared I was losing everything. However the more I seemed to try to pull him closer to me the farther he pushed away. I felt so alone, I loved him so much.

Perhaps I was the catalyst to the infidelities. I guess I will never have the answer to this question. After a period of all of this self-doubt I guess I just started to believe it had to be me. Mark's friend John was making sure he was around all the time. I guess you could say they had a love hate relationship. John was always there to tell me I was beautiful, that Mark was lucky to have me, that he didn't treat me the way I should be treated. He would tell me that Mark was being unfaithful and that he didn't deserve me. He would tell me that if he was lucky enough to have me love him he would never look at another woman again. At this point John and Erin were no longer together. They hadn't dated very long but she was very hurt over the break up. After hearing this so often and for so long I guess I started to believe I had lost Mark and that it was just a matter of time until he told me he was leaving. I wondered, am I really that unattractive? Am I that undesirable? What is wrong with me?

Then came a night I regret with every ounce of my heart. Mark had gone to work angry at me again and when John came by to visit he found me in tears in the living room. He sat beside me on the couch, put his arm around me and talked quietly to me while he moved the hair from my face. I was a wreck. I felt sure it was a matter of time and I would be alone and heartbroken and there was nothing I could do to stop it. He just held me quietly while I cried. After a while John pulled me down to lay beside him on the couch. I guess it was naiveté on my part, not that this is any excuse because in hind sight it wasn't. It was the worst mistake I had ever made to this point.

I really thought he was just being a good friend and comforting me in a bad time. I thought he was a friend of Mark's as well as mine. I wasn't there for all the history between them I only knew what I had been told. After I started to calm down John leaned over me and he kissed me. I knew this was so wrong but a part of me felt so alone and I can't lie if I expect to be brutally honest when it comes to Mark's behaviour throughout this marriage. I knew this was wrong to let him kiss me but there was a part of me that just felt so alone, so sad and I needed to feel needed, needed to feel like I was good enough again and to feel desired. John told me that Mark was a lucky guy and how he couldn't understand how Mark didn't see what he had and cherish it. He told me how beautiful I was. He listened when I needed to talk and he made me feel like what I had to say mattered. Mark at this point just always seemed angry with me.

I pulled away and I told John "I can't do this, I'm sorry if I gave you the wrong impression and I have so needed your friendship but I love Mark and just can't give up on us yet". John told me he understood and he had to leave but if I ever changed my mind he was only a phone call away. Although I missed having my friend to talk to I never changed my mind. I didn't say anything to Mark because I knew we would never survive it. I just wish Mark could have looked at me like he actually saw me instead of looking through me. I never went any further than a kiss with John and I am very thankful that I had the sense to still know what was right and wrong. Nothing happened between John and I that even crossed the smallest line of friendship after that night. How could one kiss be the start of such a destructive path through my life?

I think Mark sensed that something had happened, I was not a cheater and I guess not a very good liar either. He picked up on my emotions I guess. He didn't say anything to me and it didn't come to light until about five months later. Mark and I were sitting on our front porch one night and he quietly asked me out of the blue if I had slept with John. I was quiet for a moment wondering where this was coming from and afraid to answer. I knew Mark had a temper and I knew I had no feelings for John and never did aside from friendship but I also know that I loved Mark and I didn't want to lose him.

He continued to tell me he loved me and that whatever I told him we would get through it and that I could trust him whatever it was it was in the past. I did. I told him about the night on the couch and what I felt and what I felt now. He responded in anger and there wasn't a lot of understanding at all. In fact his main concern was whether or not tongues were involved in the kiss. He didn't take it well at all. I felt like his speech to me about trusting him and if I was honest he understood it was in the past and we would get through it was nothing more than a way to get me to talk. He never meant those words at all.

I don't remember how the night ended but I do remember the next day. I was attending college at the time and I came home only to find Mark moving his dresser out of our home. I immediately started to cry and I asked him what he was doing. He told me he couldn't get past John and he was leaving. He said he had been through this with his first wife and he wasn't going through it again. I remember sliding down the wall in the hallway and crying right from my soul and begging him not to leave me and telling him how much I loved him. It took some time but he agreed to stay. I think this was the beginning of a long and painful road.

I was having such a hard time reconciling the two characters of my husband, it was like Dr. Jekyll and Mr. Hyde. There were times when he could say such hurtful things and he could make me feel so bad about myself and I remember getting to the point where I was thinking, he must be really something because all the women seem to want him and I must not be much of anything because I can't seem to hold on to him. Therefore, the only conclusion that was left for me to draw was that I was the problem. Then there was the other side of Mark, the side that I loved with every ounce of my being. The Mark that when he wanted to could make you feel like you were the only thing in the world that mattered to him. This is the side of him that keeps me loving him. The Mark that cuddles you close and tells you he loves you, the Mark that holds my hand and loves my children as his own. The Mark that makes me laugh. There are times when he hugs me and really wraps his arms around me and I feel so safe and so loved.

In time, I came to find out Mark wasn't really the forgiving type but he was the type to seek revenge. I still to this day don't think he has forgiven me for that kiss nor do I think he believes me when I say that is as far as it went. I wish with all my heart I could turn back time and take back that one moment that hurt his heart. Maybe I wouldn't be where I am today if that were only possible.

He risked loving me and I let him down just as all the women in his life so far had done. I was hoping to show him I was different, I was safe and it turns out I was weak when it came to a sore heart and I allowed myself to accept the comfort from someone that I had no right to accept it from. I reaped the rewards of my careless handling of his heart, tenfold.

Chapter Four

Revenge

Time passed and life seemed to return to normal but I felt the change in my relationship. Mark was no longer unguarded. He was more distant with me and I could feel that his heart was no longer completely mine, if it ever was.

We had another couple that was around most of the time. Wayne and Lana. Over the time Mark and I had been together Wayne and I became very good friends as were he and Mark or so I thought. Lana was someone that I managed to get along with but she always left me with a feeling of unease. In time I came to find out that my intuition was correct and I only wish that I had distanced us from her long before I did.

Mark and I were at a local bar, which we frequented with our friends and Wayne and his fiancé Lana had just broken up and she arrived at the bar. Wayne was there with us and given the circumstances you can imagine things didn't go all that smoothly. I remember Mark spending a great portion of the evening outside in the parking lot consoling Lana. I went out a few times and asked him if he was coming back in only to be told in a minute. At the end of the evening Mark and I went home and all seemed normal. When I got into bed Mark said he had drank too much and couldn't lay down yet, that he was going for a walk and would I go with him. I told him didn't feel great and I was going to stay home. If only I had made a different choice.

I was still awake off and on and at about 5:00 in the morning Mark was still not home. I was concerned and went for a walk to see if I could find him. I didn't find him and came back home, not very happy at this point. He eventually came home about 6:30 in the morning. He told me he walked around and that he spent a few hours sitting at the local store just chatting with the police. We are from a small town as I noted before so everyone knows everyone. A part of me doubted his story but I wasn't to find out what really happened until sometime later.

At the time I told Mark about John we lived in a rented house in town and my niece Barb lived with us. She had a baby girl named Michelle and we were all pretty close. There were a lot of times that I was jealous because Mark and Barb seemed to be forming their relationship with each other and Michelle and it really felt like myself and my two boys were on the outside. I grew very concerned when I asked Mark one day if he thought he could ever care more for Michelle than he did for my two boys who considered him to be dad, and his response to me at the time was "I don't know". Let me tell you that is something the heart feels. I was concerned for my two boys who loved him. I loved my niece but I was also aware of the danger she and her daughter could cause to my family.

As time moved on Mark started driving Barb to all of her appointments and as I was attending college during the day and my husband worked at night, they spent a lot of undivided time together. They just kept growing closer by the day.

Life seemed to settle down somewhat although Mark was still never without his guard up with me and it was always palpable. We decided to move and start new somewhere else.

That year Mark and I bought our first home together. I was still attending college and my niece Barb came with us and rented the downstairs for her and her child Michelle.

We found a home in a small town about a half hour from where we previously lived. It was in a quiet subdivision and we moved in with happy thoughts and hopes for a new beginning where we could leave all the baggage behind.

Barb and I had always been very close and I thought she was someone I could trust with my life. I soon came to realize I had underestimated the power of lust and love. As time progressed, Mark and Barb grew closer. Mark was very attached to her daughter and he seemed to relate with her very well. I felt like the outsider. My husband works nights mostly so when I was at school he would spend his days with Barb and the baby. I noticed a change in their relationship as time progressed. They would talk for hours about everything. No matter what subject Mark wanted to talk about Barb always took a keen interest and gave him her undivided attention. It got so that when I was in school no matter where he went

Barb went with him. She always made him feel very needed both by her and her daughter. Mark has always had a soft spot for the underdog, the woman in need of help. Barb picked up on this very early in. When I mentioned how close they were getting Mark would point out that I was just being jealous and seeing things that weren't there. Around this time Mark and I stared to argue on a regular basis. I just couldn't do anything right. I thought I was just in the way and maybe I should leave and the two of them would be happier but I couldn't do it, I loved him.

He and I started to argue about the simplest things and Barb was apparently the one he talked to about how he felt and I came to find out after that she always sided with him and made him feel good.

There was one point in time where Mark's mother after visiting with Mark, Barb and the baby at her home told my husband that he was living with the right woman and sleeping with the wrong one. Mark's mother had never accepted me in his life and was very vocal about letting me know how she felt. When I heard this I felt so hurt. Why couldn't she see how much I loved him and was she seeing something that I had missed? Was she right? Mark had been making a habit of while I was in school taking Barb and Michelle to visit with him mom. I guess she picked up on the chemistry between them as well.

After a lengthy period of arguing I could tell that Mark didn't seem to feel the same way about me that he did and that it was Barb he wanted to spend his time with but at no time did I ever think that anything had actually happened between them. To me she just wasn't his type and she was my family so I thought I was safe and maybe he was right I was just being paranoid and jealous.

Then Barb dropped the bomb. We were out at the mall one day and I told Barb that I was so tired of the fighting and that I just had this feeling deep inside me that there was someone else. She told me at that time that she could tell me some things that would make me leave but that she didn't want me taking Mark's side and she would have nowhere to go. I told her that she couldn't just say something like that and then leave me hanging with my imagination. I wanted to know what she knew that I didn't but there was a part of me that felt sick at the thought of what it might be. She proceeded to tell me that Mark had been flirting with her for some time now.

Barb also told me that Mark had said that I always had to make such a big deal out of sex and that it could never just be a quickie. Apparently she told him how she likes quickies and how men need them. At that time apparently Mark told her "great when I come home from work I can sneak into your room for a quickie before I go upstairs to sleep, that way I can have my mistress downstairs and my girlfriend upstairs." She led me to believe that she was offended by his advances. She told me that when she went to get allergy testing done and he took her to her appointment and that when the nurse told her to get changed he didn't leave the room but was watching her as she changed. She led me to believe it was her he wanted and not me.

She also told me that when he took her to have her allergy tests done the doctor had told her to change into a gown and Mark stayed in the room while she changed and when she looked over her shoulder she saw him watching her with a look of lust.

I was so distraught at this point. I had my thoughts that there was someone else and I knew the two of them were getting very close but I thought I could trust her more than anyone in my life. We had been through so much growing up. I also thought Mark was a flirt but it sounded to me like my women's intuition was right on the money. He did have feelings for my niece and he was starting to suggest acting on it. Where did that leave me and my children? I was so angry and so hurt I didn't know what to do with myself. I did the wrong thing.

Rather than go home and talk to Mark about what I had been told, when I arrived home I was so hurt and so angry that he would do this to me that I went into our bedroom where he was asleep and I watched him for a moment. I was so angry at that moment I couldn't see the love. I think looking back on my actions I wanted to do something drastic as I so needed him to act on it and stop me and tell me how much he loved me and needed me. That is not how this interaction turned out.

I remember getting two garbage bags and going into our room and I started packing his clothes from the closet. He woke up and I remember him saying to me "what are you doing?" with a confused look on his face. I get now that I handled this entire situation so very wrong but as I am sure some of you out there can relate at a time like this where your heart is so bruised you don't really act on logic rather you act on nothing but emotion.

I remember saying to him in such anger "you know what Mark, you can have any woman you want, but you can't have me". He didn't say much he just got out of bed and got dressed. I told him what Barb had said to me and he seemed angry, he said she was just trying to get him kicked out so she and Michelle would be in a better position. We argued for about an hour, most of the time with me in tears. Mark didn't show a lot of emotion. I remember him turning his back to me and facing my dresser and he said "you know if you're going to kick me out you might as well kick me out for something I did do."

I had no idea what he was talking about but I do know that my stomach fell to the floor and my heart wasn't long to follow. He proceeded to tell me that he slept with someone else. I always knew that Mark was a flirt and he liked to talk a lot but I really never in a million years would have thought he would be unfaithful. I guess I thought this because things had gone so badly in his first marriage and I know how hurt he was when his wife was unfaithful so I thought he valued fidelity.

Well let me tell you when you hear those words it is amazing what the body can do. I felt like I just kept hearing them as an echo. I looked at him and it was like it was tunnel vision. I thought wow I guess I was right in thinking there was someone else. My intuition was right. On the other hand my mind was racing. I thought he had feelings for Barb and if he didn't act on it with her then that meant there was also someone else. How many women were there? I knew I had to find out who this woman was or I would start to suspect every woman in my life and I knew I couldn't live that way. I questioned him for a while but he wouldn't say. Finally I guessed the right one.

Well after questioning Mark and finding out that the woman he had slept with was Lana I was sick to my stomach. I couldn't breathe, my world suddenly got very small. I asked him when it happened and he said a while ago, it was that night after the bar when I went for a walk. Then I started to remember as much as I wanted to forget.

It is strange how the brain responds to news such as this. All I could see in my mind was him touching her, him sliding inside her. I envisioned him kissing her lips and him doing all the tender intimate things that belonged to us with her. It made me feel faint and physically ill. It was a picture I just couldn't get out of my head or my heart. If only I had known that night what I now knew I would never have left his side.

Apparently he went to Lana's house and she told him that she knew for a fact that I was sleeping with John. This of course was nowhere near the truth. Mark believed her, especially after I had told him about the kiss so I guess maybe in part I deserved this. How I wish he would have chosen to believe me. She presented herself as such a friend to him, she caressed his hair and she kissed him and eventually that night she had sex with him. I woke up that morning about 5:30 am as I said earlier and Mark was not home. When he did come home I was angry but what could I say I had no idea at the time he was in bed with someone else. Our friend's ex fiancé at that.

After Mark told me this he took his bags and as he was leaving, I remember sitting on the stairs of our new home and crying so quietly and I remember telling him how sad I was that I would never again feel his arms around me while we danced. He said "you never know". Then he left and I felt like my life had just walked out the door. I remember thinking what an odd thing to think about at that point in time, dancing. But I also remembered how when he held me in his arms and danced with me the world no longer existed it was just him and I.

Chapter Five

Aftermath

Mark left that day and it wasn't ten minutes after he left that I knew this so was not what I wanted. I immediately fell apart. I always thought if a man ever cheated on me that would be it. He would be gone and I would move on. I found out rather quickly that this was not to be the case.

This is where things from a logical person's perspective stop making sense. Let me tell you through this period of my life I was the farthest thing from logical. It was like as soon as he walked out that door I began to panic.

At the time this all occurred, I was still attending college and I had taken my OSAP loan and used it as the down-payment for our new home so I didn't have an income at the time. When Mark left he and his mother went to the bank the next day and he changed all of the accounts so that I would no longer have access to the funds to pay the bills. He left me with the house but he also left me with the bills for the mortgage, food, utilities, loans and credit cards. He didn't offer to pay anything and he knew there was access to money. He didn't seem to think about the kids living there and that I had one month left of college. The transmission on my car went that week and I couldn't afford to fix it. I dropped out of college as I had no other option. I was very shocked that he would put the kids and I in a position such as this because he was angry.

I never understood how much is involved when it comes to the one person who you believe you will spend the rest of your life with sleeps with someone else. I was so hurt and devastated and yet on the other hand I missed him terribly and wanted nothing more than for him to come home and I spent the next four months begging him to do just that. It is amazing actually when I look back on it. I totally put aside what he had done, took the blame for any problems in our relationship and promised anything I could think of to get him to come back to me.

It may not be something someone that has never gone through this will ever understand and maybe some of you that have gone through this won't understand it either. I was shocked at my behaviour myself. All I knew was that I needed him to come home. I was willing to forgive anything to make that happen.

Mark didn't really accept any responsibility for this infidelity he just blamed me for the fact that it happened. He said if I hadn't messed around with John none of this would have taken place. As time went on I started to find out more and more. I found out that he was meeting her for lunch and they would talk on the phone. My husband as I said earlier drives transport and I found out he had taken her a few times with him to Montreal. This finally brought very much to the forefront of my being that this wasn't a one night stand. This was a full blown affair, one that involved his heart as well as his pride. I talked to her on the phone and she told me about going with him on one of his runs. I talked to a friend who said he saw her in his truck with him and that Mark had stopped to talk to him and didn't seem to feel the need to hide her. I found out that Mark had called her at her home and asked her to go with him and arranged for her to meet him for the trip. It wasn't a spur of the moment thing, it was planned.

The emotions that I went through were shocking even to me. I thought that I was a stronger person than I turned out to be. I was ashamed of myself and the fact that I was so weak that I would beg him to come home after what he had done. I was angry that he wasn't ashamed of his behaviour and he didn't seem to feel bad about what he had done. Instead, he seemed to feel justified like I deserved what I got. I kept thinking about him and her for a long time. I imagined him at her home that night, I imagined her kissing him. I imagined him touching her body and caressing her tenderly. I wondered what he said to her and she to him. I wondered how much he cared for her. I wondered how close I had come to losing him to her. If she had genuinely wanted him, would he have left me for her? I believe he would have. It really hurt to think that he could care for someone else.

When I talked to Mark about it later and he said it was over, I asked him why it ended. He told me that when they were on their way home from one of those trips she looked at him and said "I can't wait to rub this in Janet's face". That would be me. He said at that moment he realized she wanted to get even with me for something and he realized it wasn't really him she cared about and he said that is what ended it.

It was so hard to accept that someone else had taken a piece of his heart. I felt so scared and insecure. Here I had Barb telling me he was interested in her and finding out he was having an affair with an ex friend. I think this was the first time in my life that I really started to doubt myself as a woman. I wondered what was wrong with me, what did they have that I didn't? I thought he loved me. I spent a lot of time during that four month period crying. I lost a lot of weight and went down from 120 pound to 104 pounds. I really didn't think I could survive without him. I wasn't there for my two boys like should have been. He was all that mattered.

I thought I had already experienced the worst pain I could ever feel. When I went to bed at night it really set in that I had lost him. It was one of the weakest times in my life so far.

I know this sounds totally absurd but when I crawled into my bed at night and he wasn't beside me and I had to face the fact that I was alone and that he was never coming back to me, that I would never feel his arms around me again and that he was really gone, reality had never been more in my face. At that moment I realized I didn't care what he had done, all I knew for sure was that I knew I couldn't survive without him so when I awoke the next morning I was on a new path. I somehow managed to take all the hurt and the infidelity and put it in a neat little box and focus on my relationship. So for the next two months I did nothing but try to get him back.

It is amazing to what depths you will allow yourself to sink when your heart is broken. I am so ashamed of my behaviour during this period of time. I couldn't eat and I was losing weight way to fast. I was on medication and all I did was cry all the time. Nothing else existed for me but the pain of him not being there. I wasn't there for my boys and they needed me. I was just totally a vacant shell. The boys started turning to Barb when they needed something because emotionally I just had nothing to offer. I had always prided myself on being an outstanding mother and nothing was more important to me than my children.

I guess it is why I find it so hard to face the fact that when my heart was broken so was everything else. I don't think I will ever forgive myself for not being there for them 100%. They deserved better than what they were getting. Twice now I had taken away what to them was dad. What kind of person does that? They had lost their step-dad too but I didn't stop and think about that all I was consumed with was getting him back. This isn't an easy thing to admit to anyone let alone write for the entire world to see.

I was a failure in my own eyes. I guess I am just hoping that reading my story and hearing the emotions and hurt that I went through you may just be a little gentler on yourself. That was a lesson I didn't learn, rather than be gentle on myself and give myself time to heal and give Mark time to miss me and me time to forgive, I dove right in and blamed myself for everything as long as it would bring him home.

I tried everything I could think of to get him back. I would beg him to call me and sometimes he would and sometimes he would just not call at all. I even took pictures of myself naked and left them in his truck along with a letter so that he would find them when he got to work thinking that maybe then he would miss me. I told him in the letter that for me it was easier for me to accept what he had done than it was for me to live without him. I even went to his place of work one night when I knew he was scheduled to come in. It was raining out and I showed up in high heels and a long trench coat and nothing else on underneath. I actually tried to use my body to get him to come back to me. I remember being so scared he would reject me and being so ashamed of myself at the time yet still unable to stop my actions. This was a time in my life where self-pride didn't exist for me.

Mark never apologized for his infidelity. He never once said he was sorry I had been hurt or that I didn't deserve it. Through this entire mess he always acted as though he was totally justified in what he had done. He never once said he would earn my trust back or that he had anything to make up for. He blamed me for his cheating. He told me that he did it to get even with me for John. He told me he wanted me to find out so that I would kick him out because he knew that was the one thing I wouldn't accept in a relationship. I tried again to explain that I never slept with John but there was no getting him to believe me. It hurt that the man that said he loved me was capable of such a destructive act towards me and could seek such revenge against me and yet still say he loved me. The depth of the hurt and betrayal was so deep.

During this time of trying to get my husband back, I was given more news to digest and forgive. I thought that his infidelity with Lana was the only thing I had to deal with. I was wrong.

I found out that before Mark slept with Lana there was a night when he was on his way to work and had taken his truck and went to pay a visit to our friend Erin at her apartment. He told her that he knew that I had slept with John when they were dating and that he wanted to get even and he wanted to know if she wanted to get even as well. He suggested they sleep together. Now hearing this just confirmed what I had thought before and that was that Mark had always been attracted to Erin and I guess now he felt that he had the perfect excuse to satisfy that curiosity. Erin told him no but her reasons were not what you would expect to come from a friend. I guess if it had been me that was approached by a friend's partner and asked such a question the answer to me would have been easy and simple. "No way and you should be ashamed of yourself for even asking such a thing and I would suggest you go home and tell your partner, my friend, because I intend to tell her immediately what you have suggested". This was not what happened. Erin told Mark that no, she wouldn't sleep with him but her reason was that she didn't want to be a one night stand. It hurt to hear that because the thoughts that went through my mind were wow if he told her he was leaving me and wanted her would her answer have been different and why didn't she tell me he had been there. I came to realize at that moment that she really wasn't a friend to me at all and our friendship drifted and has never returned. Apparently when he was leaving she walked him to the door and they kissed at her door for some time. Now I'm sure you are wondering how I came to hear this part of the story. Before Barb left our home she called Erin on the phone and got her to talk about it while I listened on the other end. So there was no room for doubt, what I had heard was true.

I remember thinking to myself, how many times does it take to finally get even enough. I could understand and wrap my heart around the fact that maybe he believed I had slept with someone else and maybe he believed he had the right to get even. But that only explained the one infidelity after that there was nothing to get even for, it was nothing more than an affair at that point. It was no longer about revenge, it had become something more.

There was one night when Mark agreed to come over for dinner and I had typed up a contract, which was another desperate attempt on my part to get through to him. I made it like a joke with things like: I promise to start your every day with a smile and I promise to watch all your science shows with you and stuff like that and I promised at the bottom to make sure he would never regret coming home because I would show him how good we could be and I signed it. I had a line for him to sign that he would come home but he never did sign it.

Mark moved home after about four months of being apart and I remember being so relieved. Barb moved away with her daughter so it was Mark and me and our two boys together again. I thought the worst was behind me.

I never knew until that moment how very reliant I was on having a man in my life. I looked around at independent people and would wonder how they did it. I just couldn't seem to get there. Mark wasn't very kind during this time. He was very angry at the way that I had told him to leave and he totally lost focus on the infidelity and it became all about me being wrong and having to convince him I was worth his coming home. I promised to change, to not be jealous and I promised this wouldn't haunt our relationship. Eventually Mark came home.

I was so happy to have him there and all was great for a short period of time until we started getting back into the routine of life. It was at this time that the ghosts started making their appearance. I was able to relax a little because I had him home and I was very careful to try to be what I thought he wanted me to be in order for him to be happy. On the other hand, I felt the hurt and the anger begin to surface. I thought I was ok with everything but as time went on the questions surfaced.

When Mark decided to move back in, I asked him for his little black book so I could put all of his numbers back in the phone for him. He really seemed resistant to me getting my hands on this little black book which of course raised all kinds of red flags for me. Wayne was visiting and he went out to Mark's jeep and brought in the book for me and handed it to me and let me tell you Mark did not look at all impressed. I quickly figured out why he didn't want me to have the book. Lana's phone number was in his book where it hadn't been before. He tried to tell me that it was there before when she was living with Wayne but I knew that it wasn't. I believed he was still seeing her, or at least he was still in contact with her and again, or so it felt to me, I was still the other woman. Mark told me that his night with Lana was only a one-time thing and it happened that night at her apartment. He never would admit he cheated or that it was an affair. He still says he didn't have an affair.

This changed a very big part of me. I became over vigilant. I became suspicious and I became subservient. I was previously a person that what witty and strong and very out spoken about what I needed in a relationship. From this moment on all of that changed for me. I lost what self-confidence I had and I didn't know how to get it back or if I could get it back. I became more quiet and afraid to say what I felt in fear he would leave me.

Chapter Six

The Tidy Little Box

A while after Mark moved back in and we got back into a routine of life, that little box that I had so neatly tucked away started to haunt me. I guess I never really took the time to deal with any of the hurt over his infidelity. There was a lot of hurt there. I never thought Mark would carry through and sleep with someone else and the pictures were still in my mind daily. I wanted so desperately to believe he was just a flirt with everyone. I knew in my heart that I wasn't the one that made him cheat but this was still what I was being told. In reality, he had an interest in her and he just had a good excuse to cheat and follow through with any curiosity he had about her, and blame me. He stuck with that story. Actually he still sticks to that story today.

If there is one thing I have learned the hard way, it would be that no one, absolutely no one makes a man cheat. He makes that choice all by himself and when he looks in the mirror the morning after it is himself that he needs to blame. Any carnage that follows his actions are his and his alone to clean up.

It wasn't long after Mark moved back home that we went out to the bar with friends. Lana showed up at the bar and I know I should have behaved like the adult that I was supposed to be. Any of you women out there that have been in my shoes, I'm betting you can totally relate. When you are face to face with the woman who was in bed with your man all sense of maturity goes completely out the window.

Of course while she was standing up at the bar I had to go and order a drink and have something to say. Well let's just say I wasn't at all flattering when I spoke with her. It came to my attention that Mark called her the next day to apologize for my behaviour. Let me tell you does that ever send your blood pressure through the roof. Here I was facing the woman he had an affair with and as far as I was concerned I had every right in the world to be angry and say whatever I felt I needed to say to her and if anything he should have stood behind me and had a little compassion and understanding but no he chose to side with her and call her to make sure I looked the fool. Again another hurt to overcome. Even though he had promised me that he would have no contact with her again, he called her to apologize for me.

Around this time Mark's mother went into the office where Lana worked and she told Lana that she could understand why Mark wanted to be with her. I was really getting to a point where I just couldn't take any more. Was I the only one on this planet that thought what he did was hurtful and wrong? Was I really that bad of a spouse that I really did deserve all of this? Had I asked to be betrayed? What was so wrong with me?

I found out later that Lana had an abortion about the time that Mark moved back home. At the time she was seeing Mark she was living with a man that had had a vasectomy so she couldn't tell him that she was pregnant. I also found out from Wayne that Mark had called Lana to see that she was all right after the abortion. This was after he promised me he would have no contact with her. I asked him why he called and he said he felt bad for her and that this was something that would be hard for any woman and that he was being compassionate. I don't think he realized the message that he sent directly to my heart and soul. In my heart I felt sick, I asked him if he had used a condom when they had sex and he said yes. However, there was a huge part of me that believed this child was his, otherwise, why would he have been concerned for her well-being? This is one of those questions that I will never have the answer to.

When Mark and I first met he knew that I had two boys and that I had had my tubes tied and could have no more children. I knew it was a huge sacrifice on his part to get involved with me knowing that he would never have biological children of his own. Thankfully he said he loved me enough that it didn't matter to him. So when I heard the news about the abortion and heard about Mark calling her I was left with no other choice about what to believe. I truly believe the baby was Mark's. I also believe they discussed the abortion and how she couldn't tell her spouse. I think he supported her in her decision and wanted to make sure she was all right. It has been years since this took place and you know there are still times where something will happen to trigger the thoughts of her and the baby. I wonder if he wishes he was with her and had that child. I wonder if he ever thinks about the baby. He adamantly denies that it was his.

I was too afraid to make a big deal about it because I thought that if I did I would lose him and the one thing that I knew for sure was I didn't want to go back there. I didn't think I would make it if I did. I felt that I had no choice but to accept that he had called her whether I liked it or not.

It also came to light that when he was seeing Lana and he took her with him in his transport to Montreal they had stopped at a truck stop and had sex. Mark used to take me to this truck stop for breakfast whenever I went with him. Once I found out she was there with him I haven't been back since, it actually took me quite a while before I was even able to go in the truck with him that it didn't haunt me every time. I would look at the bunk and I would see him in there with her. I would wonder if she was better company than I was. I would wonder if he wished things had turned out different between them. I wondered if he regretted his choice to be with me. I wondered did she start the physical when they were in the truck or did he just pull over and take her to the bunk. I wondered crazy things like did she perform oral sex on him while he was driving. Did she give him good memories? She must have been doing something right because he continued to see her and have sex. Mark told me he thought Lana really cared about him. I think there is a lot more to their story but I will never know all of it. In my heart I believe he had genuine feelings for her and for him it was a beginning of something. I think if she hadn't said that she wanted to rub it in my face that he may have eventually left me for her. I may be wrong but again it is just one of those scenarios that you can never find the answer to but the doubts when you think about it will always be there.

I remember how I never found any resolution to the issues surrounding Mark and Barb. It all kind of got put on the back burner when Lana came into the limelight.

After Mark moved home I guess you could say that everything that was packed so nicely into my tiny little box continued to come unraveled.

Barb and Mark weren't speaking, both blaming the other for the outcome. I of course was in the middle, both were telling two completely different stories and Mark was my partner and Barb was my niece. I knew from history not to just blindly believe Mark and but I didn't see Barb as an innocent in the entire mess either. Mark said he would do whatever he could to prove to me that nothing happened between them and that Barb was lying.

So hearing this, I thought I would jump on the opportunity while it presented itself. I went out to the local Radio Shack and purchased a very small tape recorder that would fit in someone's pocket. I took it home and I asked Mark to go and visit Barb on the premise of fixing things within the family. I told him I needed him to ask her a lot of questions about the things she said. He looked a little nervous and he told me if he did this he would have to lie to get her to answer the questions which may implicate him. He reluctantly agreed to do this for me. I knew he had to put in that disclaimer because there would be two voices on that tape and one was going to be Barb giving her side. She would also have no reason to lie as she would believe the conversation was between the two of them and in that it was the two of them that had started a relationship be it physical or not they could talk between themselves honestly or so she would think.

Mark dropped me off at a local donut shop and went to see Barb at her apartment. She believed I was at a doctor's appointment and he had to pick me up later. Well after the niceties were out of the way and they got to the real issues, basically what I found out was that they both had developed feelings for each other. Mark was reluctant to admit this, as he knew I would hear the tape but from what Barb had to say I knew it was true.

She admitted she found him very attractive and that she had thought about sleeping with him and she said "but Mark you can't say you weren't thinking the same thing, because you told me you were." She said how he would always ask her to show him her breasts. She said that they had discussed her having another baby and that he could be the father and that way if anything ever happened between myself and Mark I could never take that baby away from him because it would be his. They talked about how he was always hurt by the fact that he didn't have any biological children and when he met me that was no longer a possibility and she could give him that because she knew by what he had told her that this was something he wanted. He said well of course he had thought about it. He told her he wished that Michelle was his and that he had met her first.

She said that Mark had told her before that he no longer even found me attractive and that he thought I looked like planet of the apes when I smiled. I knew she wasn't lying about this because this is something he had said to me on a few occasions that I looked like planet of the apes but I must say I never once thought he no longer even found me attractive. She went on to say that he had said the only reason he was still with me is because I provide him with a good life, he liked having someone cook for him and clean his clothes and he didn't have to be alone. The hardest part of hearing your soul mate doesn't find you attractive any longer is getting the thought out of your head. If he felt that way once what could possibly make you believe that now he has changed his mind and he thinks you're beautiful which is what you were hoping he thought of you all along.

They discussed how they had talked seriously for quite some time about sleeping together and even broached the subject of him coming downstairs when he got home from work for a quickie while I was at school. She talked about how he told her that whenever he had sex with me I had to make such a big production of it all, with the candles and stuff and he always felt like he had to perform and how she wouldn't make him feel that way. This hurt to hear especially since I was trying so hard to keep his desire alive and I really didn't stand a chance in hell because his desire was totally absorbed in another direction, hers. He had been having troubles with his illness and his sex drive so I thought if I tried harder to set the mood it would help us reconnect on a passionate level. So yes that hurt to hear and I haven't even attempted candles and music or anything else since. It would just be a reminder, so I let him take the lead. That way I know that in my heart I am not leading him somewhere he will tell some woman later he didn't want to be. It is just safer that way.

They both admitted that they had feelings for each other and how they had talked about how they wished that Barb had met him before I did.

I knew in my heart that there was more between them than friendship, I knew it in my soul, and now I guess I had heard it from their own mouths. You know you can't ever get any kind of peace until you think you have found out everything that there is to find out and then when you do you end up wishing you knew nothing.

So when it is all said and done it really is a no win situation for the one that has been cheated on and this I guess is a prime example of cheating without sex. It hurts just as deeply and in some ways it is a hurt that is on a different level because in an affair like this one you know the heart is involved. I think you have more of a risk of losing the man you love to an affair of the heart than you do to one that is for sex and sex only.

Why is it men can't see the writing on the wall. How can they not notice that they are developing feelings for a friend or anyone other than their wife and stop it right there and avoid that person if necessary before it goes too far? Shouldn't that be a perfect indication that it is time to spend more time with your wife and to start putting the effort into rekindling that friendship and passion instead of taking that road which will eventually destroy everything about her? I wonder, is it a lesson a man will ever learn?

In the end, my heart gets hurt and I get a little bit more broken. The answer: is illusive.

This puts me in a precarious position. I can't demand he have no female friends but on the other hand I have been shown over and over again that I can't trust him to be able to have a female friend and have it remain just that.

I can't say that it was easy getting past any of this. I think when something like this happens to you that it takes a part of you away and changes who you are and I don't think you ever go back to the person you were. I don't think that is possible.

I know I had a lot of demons to try to deal with and a lot of doubts and hurts to heal. I knew it would take some time. I found I had become ever more vigilant watching who he was talking to or how he was flirting with a certain person. I watched him around our friends. I found myself trying to look more beautiful so he would notice me and maybe not need anyone else. I walked on eggshells trying to be the perfect partner. I had my moments of weakness, as I wasn't always able to control my jealousies.

I found out that no matter how vigilant you are or how much you try to never lose your temper or show your insecurities they still have their moments of power.

There was a night at our home when Wayne brought his sister over to meet us before we were to all go out. We had never met her before and when she walked in I knew she was going to be an issue. She was the perfect description of everything my husband thinks is beautiful in a woman and everything I didn't have. She had blonde hair and blue eyes and was tall and she was very outgoing.

At the time Mark had a jeep and Wayne's sister wanted to see the jeep so she, Mark and Wayne went outside to see it. I went to the bathroom to finish my make-up and when I came out of the bathroom and walked by our front entrance I see Mark walking back into the house and he has Wayne's sister in his arms and he is carrying her and she has her arms around his neck and the two of them are laughing. I couldn't help myself, my heart plummeted and all I could think was you hurtful jerk, we just get back together after everything you did and you know I am in a fragile place but rather than help me through it you're on to your next conquest. I remember saying out loud to him "what do you think you're doing". He immediately got very angry at me and he put her down and said "she didn't have any shoes so I carried her in." My response was "well she managed to go out there just fine without them," and I went into the bathroom and closed the door.

I was hurt and I was crying because all the ghosts came back to me and all of a sudden she was Lana or at least the next Lana and I still wasn't enough. Mark came into the bathroom and left the door open so everyone out there heard every word he said to me. He was very angry and not at all in an understanding place. He said to me "if you don't get a hold of your jealousies I am not going to put up with this, I will leave you, do you hear me? I will leave you." I remember looking at him with tears on my face and I said ok and I looked down at the sink. He left the bathroom and I didn't mention it again.

It is amazing when you are afraid of losing someone that you think you need just to survive what you are willing to accept. When I think of the hurtful words that he would say to me and how I was at fault because he chose to have an affair and here I was willing to just say ok and not argue because I really felt that this was the only way I was going to keep him.

He wasn't always hurtful and mean but these are the emotions that go hand in hand with the infidelity. He was caught cheating and he didn't like that there was a mess to clean up after it all came out in the open. He didn't want his life to change and he wanted the trust and he wanted the freedom to keep flirting with the girls and he didn't seem to grasp that his choice to cheat is what changed all of that.

Chapter Seven

Parties

Some time had passed and things started to get a little better and over time I started to rebuild a little faith. It seemed Mark and I had turned a corner and we had found a place of happy at least that is my perspective. Mark asked me to marry him. Now in our past, Mark had asked me to marry him six different times so when he asked me this time I immediately said "don't you dare ask me this again unless you are willing to sit down and set a date today." He smiled and hugged me and well, we set a date.

I spent the next few months planning our wedding and if I must say so myself it was the most beautiful wedding ever. We were married outside in a rose garden with friends and family present. My boys were a big part of all of it. I remember walking down the aisle thinking happily to myself. He loves me. He said he would never get married again but he loves me and here he is. I was sure the days of Mark and women were over, he would never have married me if he wasn't 100% sure I was the one he wanted.

After the wedding we were good for a long time. We had reached an understanding on so many points and life was good.

Then there came the bomb again. We had these two, for me acquaintances, but for Mark she was an ex- girlfriend and he was a friend. Their names were Todd and Marianne. They came over one night for drinks and to hang out which was odd in the first place but I was ok with it. I knew he didn't have any residual feelings for her as he never developed any while they were dating. During the evening Mark, Todd and Marianne were drinking. I couldn't drink at the time as I had stomach issues that prevented me from consuming alcohol.

At one point in the evening Mark asked Todd if he would like to go downstairs to see the models that the kids had built and Todd said sure so they left Marianne and myself alone to talk. Now Marianne was a real partier and she and Todd were also into drugs on a social level. I knew she had experienced women sexually as well and she started talking about that and asking me if I had ever experimented with women. I told her no and then Todd and Mark came back upstairs. Apparently while they were downstairs they had arranged an experience for me. I was still in that place where I was very afraid to say no to anything Mark asked of me. He said he wanted to see me with a woman and remember during all of this I was sober. He asked me to lie naked on the living room floor and Marianne proceeded to start to kiss me while Todd gave me oral sex in front of Mark. It was horrible. I did not find Todd at all attractive and the only man I wanted touching me was my husband. It was like an out of body experience for me is the best way to describe it. I had to get out of myself in order to get through it. The only way I could think of to get Todd away from me was to fake an orgasm so I did and that ended that part. I immediately got up and said I have to go to the bathroom and I ran to the bathroom where I closed the door and cried for a few minutes and felt so dirty but I knew I didn't have much time and I would have to go back out there. So I did. When I got there Mark was touching Marianne and said Todd would be with me. I walked over to Todd and was told to put baby oil on his penis and jerk him off before he had sex with me. So I put the baby oil on him and he complained about the mess and he put me on my back on the floor and laid on top of me. He hadn't gotten hard yet a small favour I was grateful for. I looked over and saw Mark and Marianne having sex in front of me and I heard her say to him "I always hoped I would be with you again I just wished that I looked better when it happened." He told her she looked fine. Meanwhile Todd was grinding on top of me trying to get hard and couldn't. I looked over at Mark and finally got his attention because he and Marianne were finished and I mouthed the words "help me". He immediately got up and told Todd that was enough this was over.

I ran to the couch and I huddled in the corner with my knees drawn up to my chest. I was somewhere else. Mark got Todd and Marianne to leave and I remember him coming in the living almost yelling "I just wrecked everything didn't I, I ruined everything." I couldn't talk. He came over to the couch and went to hug me but I just couldn't let him touch me. I felt so dirty I couldn't even put it into words, I felt used and the only way I can describe it is I had all the emotions I can imagine a rape victim going through only there thank god was no penetration.

Mark tried to soothe me for about four days but I just couldn't be touched. All I could see was Todd touching me, I could feel his hands on my body every time Mark touched me. Mark told me we had to take it slow but I had to let him touch me and get me past this so I tried. Eventually I got ok with his touch again. I still can't listen to the song by smashmouth that played over and over that night. It was Todd's favourite song. I couldn't believe Mark would put me in such a horrible position knowing he was the only man I wanted ever. We never saw Todd and Marianne socially again but did hear in the not too distant future that Todd had HIV and so did Marianne. Thank God for small favours.

It came time that we sold our house that we had bought a few years back and decided to build one from scratch. It was a happy time building the house and I really felt that the worst was behind me I mean what worse could possibly happen, I had been through it all right? After all the hard work we had finally made it. The boys were happy and we were starting to have a great social scene and we had the house with the perfect rec room for entertaining. We bought a pool table and built the bar and got the great stereo to boot.

Over the next few years there were a few bumps in the road but I always put it down to Mark's wild side. He was always a very sexual person and he liked to play. We went through a period in our marriage however that I am not very proud of.

I was always afraid in the back of my mind that I had to be all that I thought Mark needed me to be so that he would love me and stay with me. I started thinking not very rationally and I thought well if there are moments when I give him some treats then he won't sneak around and have an affair. So we started having parties at our home and I started to drink quite a bit of wine. I found that when I was drinking wine I wasn't so shy and Mark seemed so much happier with this person than he did with the sober me. All sounds pretty normal doesn't it? Not even close.

It got so we were partying all the time. It was nice to have friends around and Mark seemed to really love this side of me. He was attentive and loving and I thought finally I'm making him happy. We were both enjoying the social time where everything seemed to be happy. There was no stress in our lives and all was good.

Well the parties started to progress as time went on. Eventually we would play games. We would have games of pool and the loser would do a lap dance on someone at the party. Everyone thought this was a great time and it was fun. Over time it started to get more risqué. Mark was very flirty with the girls at the party and eventually at these parties it got to the point where the girls would give my husband oral sex while he laid on the pool table and I got to take pictures. It wasn't a long event just long enough for him to experience the taboo of it and get his fix or so I thought. This is so wrong on all levels.

I don't even know what I was thinking when I look back on it now. I am certainly not proud of myself, in fact I am outright ashamed of my behaviour and my reasons for thinking what I was thinking. I remember being there yet it was like I was off in a tunnel. I remember taking those pictures and the tears silently running down my cheeks as I watched. He seemed happy and the girls didn't seem to mind. I never touched another man nor did I ever even consider giving anyone oral sex. Mark is the one I wanted. I guess deep down inside every time he was offered someone a part of me was so desperately waiting to hear those words come from his heart "thanks but I have everything I want right here." Those words never came.

I think sad as it sounds that during my twenty years with Mark it was during this time period that he was most happy. I remember being at a local trucker's office one day that Mark knew and he told this man that he didn't have to cheat that his wife lets him have favors at home. Well between the two guys they thought this was just too cool. Now I must take blame where I deserve it. I told Mark that I was totally ok with all of this. I told him that he could do this and it was all just in fun. It was when I was alone and I couldn't hide from me that the truth was unavoidable. Deep down I really believed that this was the only way to keep him and him be happy. I truly believed that he would never be happy and content with only one woman. I guess as illogical as all of this may sound I thought that the demons I could see would be easier to accept than those that were behind my back.

You know that after all we had been through so far, I really must be a slow learner because I must give credit where it is due and put the blame where it belongs because Mark never asked for any of these extras. He just never turned them down either. Why did I keep offering him all of these play things knowing how much it was going to hurt? Because I have always believed that I never have been nor ever will be enough for him to be happy and for him to be faithful. The hardest part of having to watch this take place was that the women doing this to my husband were my girlfriends. I got very confused about what a friend was supposed to be because in my mind a friend would never touch another friend's husband no matter whether he was offered or not.

As I read over these words years later I am left with such a sad feeling. How does a girl who grew up so confident that marriage was forever and that when you love someone and they love you back then you have found true happiness, end up being so emotionally damaged that I would talk myself into believing that the way to keep my own husband happy was to offer him women to play with. I don't want to sound like a victim but honestly I do feel sad for the little girl in me. I think about what my mother would have thought of my choices and my weaknesses. I discovered weaknesses in myself that I never knew I was capable of feeling.

Back to the story, there was one night during this period of parties Mark and I went to a strip bar with his nephew and his nephew's date. I don't remember her name but I do remember she was again a blonde. I noticed throughout the evening that Mark seemed very focused on her and I was a little jealous of the attention she was getting from my husband. I remember we came back to our place for a drink and we were all sitting on the couch talking. Mark thought it would be cute if the guys did a sort of strip tease dance for the girls. I thought it was cute and they put on the music. When they stood up I was in for another surprise as Mark said "hey we should switch partners". I tried to hide my hurt and not cry in front of everyone and make a fool out of myself. I do remember thinking again that it wasn't me he wanted, that he had spent the evening focusing on the new girl, the blonde hair and blue eyes and this was his way of getting to play with her. I had no interest in Mark's nephew, in fact, I have never had an interest in anyone but my husband. This was just another one of those situations where I let myself go numb. I was there but I wasn't there. I don't remember what Mark did for his dance but I do remember crying inside and yelling in my head, "get this man away from me." I also remember not being able to take my eyes off of Mark and this girl. I remember hating him at that moment. I remember once again asking myself why can't he just love me." Why aren't I good enough for him and why does he find it so easy to just hand me over to another man and feel no jealousy whatsoever?

There were a lot of little instances that were hard on my heart but after hearing something so many times, it's almost like you start to expect it and you're not really all that surprised when you hear it. Sad as that sounds it's true.

There was a friend of mine, Leslie, she did my hair at my wedding actually and she lived just down the road from where Mark works. After spending so many years with someone you can't help but learn their routine and how they handle their time off and their work time so when something happens that doesn't fit the routine you start to pay attention. At this time I was working for a lawyer in town so when Mark came home from work most days I wasn't there. He would normally come right home and sleep because he had been out trucking the entire night before.

Well one day on my lunch hour I was walking through town, it was summer, and I ran into an acquaintance on the street. She stopped me and showed me a letter she had received from John from jail. He at one point lived with Leslie. This acquaintance was also an ex of John's.

Apparently, Leslie had written to John in jail and she had told him that Mark had been stopping by to visit with her when he finished work in the morning and that he had been there to visit her three times that week. I couldn't believe what I was reading. I had known Mark for a very long time and one thing I did know was that when he is done work he is very tired and he goes directly to bed. I felt that I had again been very deceived. He hadn't told me anything about his visits which in my eyes means there is something to hide. I asked Mark about this and he told me yes he had dropped by a few times but there was nothing going on. He said he helped her move a weight bench and they just talked. He said he didn't tell me because he knew I would get mad. He said he only stopped because he knew I was at work and he wasn't tired and he didn't want to come home to an empty house.

He used to do little things that would raise red flags for me but they were things I couldn't do anything about but they certainly didn't help me rebuild any trust that's for sure. Whenever I was at work I would come home and Mark would have deleted all of the callers from the phone as well as all the numbers that had been called from our phone. However, on my days off from work he never went near the phone.

It is amazing how your heart and your mind can shift gears so quickly. I would wake up some mornings and all the hurt was in my face and then there were so many mornings where I would wake up and smile thinking about the things Mark did that were so thoughtful and loving. There were so many times when he could be everything a woman could ever want in a husband like the night when my youngest son was about five and he needed a Sheppard's costume for a school play the next day. I didn't have a clue where to even start with the project and Mark took out a blue sheet and a pair of scissors and when he was done my son was the best looking Sheppard in the play. It is those moments that the love for him is so deep.

It is a hard thing to accept when you discover that you are not capable of being independent and on your own. I look around me and so many women I know are happy being alone. I guess that is just not who I am. I wish I could be strong like my mother was and yet forgiving enough to not give up on marriage and love. I am still working on finding a balance that will allow just that but I also know that first I have to find me again and until that happens I really won't know what peace is. I have to find a way to not look for that in someone else but to find it in me and then be able to share it with someone else. I need to find a way where I won't feel responsible for the choices of the man I love. I need to find a way to believe that when he cheats it is his choice of action not something I'm responsible for or have even an ounce of control over.

There will probably be a lot of women reading this book that will experience anger towards me and that will think well if she's willing to put up with it then why wouldn't he continue to do it. She offered it so she deserves whatever she gets and if she's stupid enough to stay then I have no sympathy for her. I guess before I lived it I probably would have said or thought the same thing. Problem with that is I have learned that you don't really know what you will do or how you will react until you are living it. I have had people tell me that there must be a part of me that is defective for me to stay with him after all that has happened. Yet here I am and surprisingly enough I still love him deeply. I don't know, maybe I just can't let go of the 80% of him that is so good to me and the children just to get away from the 20% that hurts me deeply.

It has been a relationship that has been very confusing, at least to me. Even though I was the one living it and could see Mark's mood swings and his flirty behaviours so clearly, everyone I knew saw Mark as this fun loving and giving guy at all times and I felt like the nagging, jealous and controlling spouse.

After a while you start to question yourself at every turn. Is it just me he can't get along with because if he gets along so well with everyone else and I'm the only one he fights with then I must be the problem? Only now that you believe it is you that is the problem but you have absolutely no concept on what to do about it. So that was the next part of my journey.

Chapter Eight

Reality

Mark and I had reached a point in our marriage where even the day to day communication was difficult. There was a distance between us. We would argue about such superficial things that really looking back held no merit at all.

A part of my story that I should have noted earlier was that Mark and I started doing foster care for teens between the ages of 15 and 21. We usually had four foster teens at a time and my two boys who at this time were teens as well. There were many times that my friends would tell me what a great mother I was and they knew that this was where my passion had always been. They suggested I look into it and when I did, Mark and I discussed it and decided we would give it a try. We also had my youngest son's girlfriend living with us as well, so needless to say it was a pretty busy household. It was easy temporarily to put our issues aside and we became totally absorbed by all the kids. We did this for ten years before that era ended, a part of the story I will get to later.

There was a party at our house one night and we had invited a few friends that weren't regulars at our house. One was named Cindy. Mark had slept with her way before he met me when they were younger, after he separated from his first wife and was playing the field. It was a one-time thing but they remained friends. I always thought she was cute and Mark said he would like to see me play around with a woman and asked if she were here would she be someone I would consider. I was attracted to her for some reason even though I know myself well enough to know that I could never touch another female I'm just not homosexual but the thought of kissing a girl didn't seem to repulsive so again I thought it was something he wanted and said I would have drinks and see what happened, so she came out.

Once she was there I found that I just had no interest and avoided her without seeming to be rude in any way. I was just socializing with everyone that was there.

One of my foster boys, Scott, was at this party he was I think 17. Also at the party was a foster girl, Laurie, who no longer lived with me but stayed in touch, she was now about 20. I found out after the party was over that the two of them were out on the back deck and Cindy gave oral sex to Laurie in front of Scott. I was appalled that something like this took place right under my nose and I had no idea until it was too late.

Mark and I had become known in the area apparently for the parties we had. Everyone was of the opinion that we were swingers which was so far from the truth. There was no sex and no partner switching, there was nudity and lap dances and yes my husband did receive oral sex from my friends.

Well as this party progressed I remember coming down from upstairs and I looked around to see where Mark was and I saw him behind our bar with his back turned to me. I walked over and when I looked over the bar I saw Cindy giving him oral sex and he was being watched by one of her girlfriends. Now in my eyes it was one thing for me to offer him a treat of about 2 minutes on the pool table from a friend, it was a totally different story when it was behind my back and for a lot longer than 2 minutes. I was so lividly angry at that moment at both him and her. I remember saying to her "you have 30 seconds to get out of my house" and I walked upstairs to my room.

It was summer and my window was open and I could hear the two of them talking on the back deck outside my bedroom window while she waited for her cab to arrive. He was telling her how it was so unfair that I always got to have all the fun and he never got to have any. It was a very bad night. Once again he turned to someone else and once again it was behind my back.

The parties continued for about two years and eventually it all just seemed to become a blur to me. I guess that things really came to an abrupt end when one night after drinking a couple of glasses of wine, I remember going to the bathroom because I just wasn't feeling quite myself. When I got upstairs I started to sweat and to feel like I was about to pass out. At the same time I was sure I was going to throw up and had severe diarrhea as well. It just wouldn't go away and I ended up lying on the cold bathroom floor. I was so scared and yet I couldn't get off the floor to get help. Eventually my oldest son came to the door and asked me if I was ok. I quietly said no and he called 911.

It took a while for the ambulance to arrive and when the paramedics came in and saw me on the floor they turned me over and my entire front was soaked in sweat and yet at the same time I was shaking violently and was extremely cold. They took me to the emergency department at the local hospital and I was given an Ativan and an injection of gravol for the nausea. After approximately forty-five minutes it seemed to subside. The nurses told me that they believed I had suffered an anxiety attack and sent me home with instructions to call my doctor the next day.

Over the next week these attacks, as they referred to them, occurred frequently. I contacted my doctor and he ran some tests. The test results came back normal and he said there was no medical reason for these episodes and that he believed it was anxiety. He prescribed lorazapam for me and asked that I contact him if anything changed. So I went home.

These attacks were extremely frightening and I never knew when they would hit but when they did they lasted for about two hours. Given the frequency of these attacks I was unable to continue to consume alcohol and as a result of my not drinking the parties discontinued.

Looking back, I have to wonder if a part of this at least, was my subconscious minds way of delivering the message that enough was enough. I just think I was unable to continue to witness the behaviour that was taking place at these parties. I think that subliminally I believed that if I didn't drink then the parties would subside and I would no longer be witness to the women and my husband and this way he couldn't be upset with me for no longer wanting this to continue. Perhaps I am wrong in my thinking as since the end of the parties, life has had its ups and downs however, the episodes still occur only on a much less frequent scale. Mark was nothing short of supportive with what I was going through and he never complained once about the lack of social interaction. I was very impressed that it seemed to not bother him at all just being home with me. Perhaps I should have trusted that the extra female favours that I had offered to him in reality was not something that he had asked for or needed it was an assumption on my part.

As time went on, it started to become apparent that perhaps a big factor in these episodes was hormones. I believe it was and is a combination of stress and hormones, but I must say I am happy that the parties are a chapter of our lives that are now in the past. I can't really say it was the parties themselves that I found hard to handle because I enjoy a good party just as much as the next guy, but I am not sorry that since then I have not had to witness my husband in any kind of sexual encounter, no matter how small, and this has been a tremendous relief to my heart. Now I just needed to find a way too rid my heart of the ghosts.

The thing that seemed to cause a lot of conflict between Mark and I was his very apparent soft spot when it came to the girls. He just seemed to hold them to a different standard than he did the boys and they were able to get away with a lot of behaviours that I just truly believed were inappropriate, so we would argue. Maybe that is the way it is with all men, I'm not sure but for me it was a big issue.

I found as time progressed Mark and I started to argue more frequently and it just seemed to get more difficult to even communicate about small issues. I constantly kept myself in defense mode and was always ready for the hurtful words I knew we would exchange. I was not innocent when it came to the fighting and I am sure I was not the easiest person to live with at this point in my life. I guess there had just been so much negative accumulation that the reasons that I loved him seemed to get buried in the dust, sadly. I felt he was always vigilant for me to make a mistake and I felt that he was constantly correcting me when it came to parenting the kids.

I cannot say for sure if what I believed I was seeing at this point was accurate but I can say that it was my perspective at the time. It seemed that the kids would do something inappropriate and I was the heavy, I was the one to discipline and enforce the rules and Mark seemed to be given the role of friend. He would excuse away their behaviour for whatever reason and the kids would come to me and tell me that he had told them just that and then there would always be the feeling that is was him and them against me.

I was beginning to feel a lot of resentment towards Mark and I just couldn't seem to understand why it was never my perspective or point of view that he was in alignment with, and he always took the side of the kids no matter the issue. I was always coming off as the dysfunctional one with all the mood swings. It was easier for the kids to stand behind Mark because it made life a lot easier for them. I know that I could not have been right all the time but I don't think I was wrong all the time either.

Over time I came to just expect the opposition and I started to feel very alone and I felt there was no soft place to fall, no safe haven where I would find compassion and understanding and friendship. He always told me that he felt that I was a great mother and my kids were lucky that they were loved so much and yet he seemed to have no faith in my parenting abilities with these teens.

Over time I have come to discover that there was a lot of things that Mark believed that I didn't do right when I was raising my two boys, but because they were mine biologically he felt it wasn't his place to correct me. I think to this day he harbors a lot of resentment with the way I raised my kids. I don't know what to do about that because I believe I did the right thing with them and they have turned out to be very respectful and loving young men. I may have spoiled them more than I should but they were always made to behave in an appropriate way. I think rather than talk to me Mark just started to build resentments of his own and they festered over time.

Looking back and thinking things over there were a lot of things in our history that I never allowed myself to deal with, mostly because I didn't know how and it just hurt too much to dwell there so I put them aside as best I could and with the busy atmosphere in our home it was easy to avoid the real issues.

In a marriage when you start to argue so often over a period of time you emotionally get worn down and I started to feel just defeated and tired. From my perspective it just seemed that I could do nothing right. I am sure at this time Mark felt a lot of the same emotions and he probably felt like he never did anything right as well.

I remember reaching a point where I would think I know that I really love him but I really don't like him right now and when that realization came to me I was very scared. I decided to seek some professional help because if it really was me that was the problem then I needed to do whatever I could to fix me and to save my marriage. I so desperately wanted to get those feelings back that I always had for him, the passion, the love, the friendship and I just didn't know how to get there at this point. I thought maybe if I saw a therapist that he could teach me how to deal with the past hurts, the insecurity and the mistrust and if I could learn to change me then I could put us in a better place.

I went to see a psychotherapist for six visits or so and at that point I don't know if he was correct or not, but he listened to my story which of course was based on my perspective at the time and after he heard what I had to say he handed me a book about verbal abuse in a relationship.

I was very shocked at some of the answers he gave me. I took it home and read it immediately and I felt like I was in the twilight zone and I felt like I was reading my life story or perhaps that was what I wanted to see. In a way it was a good and a bad feeling. I think I grasped so tightly onto his explanation because I finally felt that I had validation that I wasn't crazy and I wasn't a miserable person and the only person on the planet that Mark couldn't seem to get along with. On the other hand I felt very sad. From my perspective at that point in time I felt so sad that the one person that I loved most in the world was abusing me and calling it love. My perspective was to change drastically in the months to come.

I remember that I thought I understood why he was doing it and I even had sympathy for the reasons but after trying this route for a while I started getting very burned out. I remember one day I had a couple of glasses of wine and I finally had the nerve to say what needed to be said for so long. I cried a lot and I let my emotions run free for the first time in a very long time, if ever. I told him how much I had been hurt during our time together and that I did realize that the past couldn't be changed but I told him that I also realized that that doesn't change the hurt that I feel. I told him how he seemed mad at me because I didn't trust him but on the other hand I had Barb, Lana, Leslie and Erin to give me reason not to. I told him I needed a best friend that I could talk to about anything and share my deepest thoughts with but that whenever I tried to talk to him no matter what the subject he always seemed to take the other side. I remember him listening and I could see the sadness in his face almost like a look of resolution and defeat. It had reached a point for both of us that whenever there were times that we had time alone together there just seemed to be this uncomfortable tension in the air. When I would think back to when we first started I never thought even in a million years that for Mark and I this would ever be possible, but here we were.

I couldn't figure out how you go from that kind of love and friendship and passion to where we seemed to be at this point and better yet, was it even possible to get a portion of that back? How do you really know if you no longer love someone and if you will ever love them again or if you are just unbelievably hurt and angry and you just don't have a lot of faith and trust left inside? Where do you go from here and how do you start to build a life full of love, friendship and trust? I seemed to have so many questions and so few answers. I didn't even know how to take that first step because in my heart and soul I believed that in order to get there I had a lot of unbelievable hurt to go through first. I honestly didn't know if I had the strength to still love him, but on the other hand I didn't know that I would be strong enough to let him go and have him never come back to me. What if I made the decision to let him go and it turned out to be the biggest mistake I would ever make in my life? What if I was to spend the rest of my life loving him and being alone and missing someone that I had let go?

We just continued living day to day both trying to get to that point where the past wasn't part of our present. Time seemed to pass and we didn't talk much about the relationship. I think maybe we scared each other by talking about ending it so we just went about our day to day lives and didn't discuss it. Things seemed to go along rather smoothly for a while.

Around this time we took in a new girl to live with us. She had just started grade nine and her name was Penny. She had blonde hair and blue eyes and she just had one of those characters that you couldn't help but love. She became part of the family very fast and just seemed to spring new life into the house.

I remember the summer when Penny was just finishing grade ten and she went to a friend's house a few hours away on vacation. Mark and I were scheduled to pick her up and when we reached the designated pick up point, Penny wasn't there. We waited for about a half hour and then called home to see if there was a reason for the delay. It was at this point we found out the Penny had been in a very serious car accident and that she was in the hospital and we needed to get there as soon as possible. We arrived at the hospital to find that Penny was in very bad shape and we ended up spending about three weeks with her at the hospital day and night.

There was a hotel across from the hospital where we slept when there was time. During this period of time which was very emotional and stressful for everyone involved, let's just say Mark was still Mark. It was as if he had the need to converse with every female nurse on the floor and it was very hard to obtain his attention. Now I understand that Mark has a very social personality, but I guess I just felt that at a time like this at least he would put his flirtations on hold. That was so not the case.

One of our foster sons, Scott, arrived at the hospital as he was dating Penny at the time. Mark, Scott and I were walking down the corridor one late afternoon and Mark pointed out to Scott that a young blonde girl was checking him out and that she was really cute. I remember having that familiar jealous twinge but didn't say much. The next day when we got on the elevator this same girl got on at the same time. I looked over at Mark to see his reaction and noticed he was about to start a conversation with the girl and honestly I had had enough of his obvious flirtation throughout our time at the hospital. I just very bluntly looked at him and said "don't you dare." He was angry with me I could tell that just by the expression on his face.

At the hotel we were staying at there was a young girl that was working reception.

She was cute, very outgoing and talkative. She and Mark seemed to hit it off right away as was usually the case. He had always had a way with women. There was a couple of nights where I would just sit in a chair at reception while I waited for the two of them to conclude their conversations. He was telling her his life story and she was telling him hers. He didn't understand my jealousy of this but then his understanding of my emotions where he and the girls were concerned was not something I usually was given. It was one of those moments where you just knew you were the third wheel. I couldn't seem to get through to him that it wasn't always necessary to get to know everyone and that sometimes for instance when you are checking into a hotel, all you need to do is be polite and take care of business and move on with your day. That it is disrespectful to your wife for her to stand waiting while you so obviously flirt with a girl. Now he would defend himself here and say he wasn't flirting he was no more than being friendly.

I tried to explain to him that just because it is his intention to be friendly does not mean that this is the impression that the other woman receives nor one that he sends to his wife. There was no doubt in my mind that had I not been there he would have asked her out for coffee to continue to get to know her, at least this was my impression. I remember how bad that made me feel about me and I wondered what she must think of me that my husband would so blatantly ignore me while chatting with her.

Then we would go to our room and he was again my husband, the man I loved. He was comforting and tender. He would tickle my back as we watched t.v. It was never in private that I lacked for his attention it was only when there was another female around that I felt that I became invisible to him. I don't even think it was a conscious thought where he is concerned it just was who he was. He didn't seem to see the harm in it and was totally convinced it was my insecurities and therefore my problem. He said I was exaggerating and just plain seeing things that weren't there.

I noticed after we came home that he was still really trying; he was being so nice to me. Penny had a long recovery and for quite some time we had to set up her bed in the downstairs rec-room as she couldn't climb the stairs. I was starting to feel that I was becoming important to him again.

On our anniversary we went back to the rose garden where we were married and we had a glass of wine and reminisced. It was just one of those amazing days. The weather was warm, we actually talked to each other, we kissed and took pictures and all was right with the world. However as was always the case with us the past always entered the conversation at some point and we would feel the distance grow again. I will admit that most times it was I who was always bringing up the past. It just seemed that I was always pushing. Mark would have been quite happy to leave the past in the past and live life for where we were at that moment. I was never really able to get there, I guess because I never dealt with the past in order to get to a place where I was no longer living it on a daily basis.

A lot of the time I think I was unable to put the past in the past because I never got any closure on any of the issues. I always wanted Mark to accept responsibility for his infidelities and to accept that his actions had deeply hurt me and that to me there was a cost. I think if I had been given some understanding and kindness for the hurt and an apology rather than to be blamed for the choices he made, I would have been in a far better place to travel the road to recovery, peace and forgiveness. In reality, it is very hard to forgive when the man that did the cheating refuses to admit he was wrong or that he had treated you unkindly.

It was very hard to find any resolution in my heart when I was so hurt by his actions but I was also hurt a second time when I was told it was my fault that any of it had happened. I don't think when this is what you are told it is even possible to start to move on because the resentment just builds. It was like he had done this and there seemed to be no cost to him because in his mind he had done nothing wrong. At least that was the picture that he presented to me. His denial was very hard to move past when you knew that what you were told about the indiscretions wasn't the truth. To accept that the man you love can say he loves you and look you directly in the eye and lie to you over and over again when he knows that you are aware of his lies and yet, he continues to lie some more and to continue with the charade, is not only hurtful but insulting.

As things started to become more and more distant between Mark and I and the arguing seemed to become a common part of our day, I started to notice that Mark was beginning to spend the majority of his day talking to Penny. I knew it shouldn't make me jealous, she was a child and we both looked at her like our daughter. But I guess because I felt like he was giving so little of himself to me that jealousy was exactly what I did feel. Now I'm sure he did find Penny much better company than I was.

I seemed to have gotten back into being that bitter angry person and I was starting to find myself being mean to Mark for no reason. It was almost like I was provoking him and not consciously aware that this is what I was doing. However, looking back from a much brighter place it is very easy to see he wasn't the only one to blame for where we found ourselves stuck at this point in time. It just seemed that I was so unhappy so much of the time that I just couldn't find it in me to be nice.

I remember Mark started spending more and more time at work and less and less time at home which only resulted in me feeling more alone. It was like a vicious circle. It just seemed that the only emotions I had at this time were resentment and anger and I didn't know what to do about it.

I remember one night Mark had asked me to wake him up around 10:00 p.m. as he had to go to work and I tried to convince him to stay in bed with me a little longer and cuddle me. He said he couldn't stay in bed or he would be late for work and he got up. I remember hearing him talking downstairs so I went down to see why he was still home and when I walked into the rec-room I saw Mark kneeling down beside Penny's bed with his elbow on her bed talking very seriously with her and his face was close to hers. I said to him "I thought you had to go to work?" He laughed and made some comment and said "ya I do, I was just talking to Penny for a minute." I was kind of hurt that he couldn't stay in bed a few minutes longer with me but talking to Penny was ok to be late for work for, and I went back upstairs to bed.

This was about 11:00 p.m. I went back downstairs around midnight and he was still talking to Penny. I said something to him that probably wasn't very nice something about "well it's nice to see you couldn't be late for work to stay with me in bed and cuddle but it's ok to be late to stay and chat with Penny." He then was visibly angry and he left for work. I remember thinking I can't allow him to get my self-control away from me like that again, I was just starting to get it back. I knew I needed to find a way to get back to the person I was just learning how to be before Penny's accident.

Where we were headed at this point in time I didn't really know. I didn't like me very much and I was just starting to wonder how anybody else could either. I didn't even know anymore what it was that I needed in order to be happy and I didn't remember how to laugh or have fun anymore. I was starting to ask myself the question when I looked in the mirror, "who am I?"

I started to sense a change in Mark when it came to the small stuff. It had always been a ritual for us that when he was leaving for work I would fix his coffee and walk him to the door and give him a hug and a kiss good-bye and I would always tell him to drive safe and that I loved him. One night when I walked him to the door for our usual good-bye and he hugged me, he rubbed my back and then played with my fingers and looked down into my eyes. My heart stopped. I felt like he had come to the realization that he had to say good-bye because we just didn't seem compatible anymore. I remember thinking, he wants to leave. I think he was tired of all of the fighting and I think he was growing very tired of my bad moods. His hug just felt like good-bye. He leaned over to me and he said "if you like tomorrow we can go for a drive and talk about us. We don't need any more of this." This really scared me but I knew he was right. These kids didn't need any more of the fighting and neither did he or I. I hadn't seen Mark happy in a long time.

I remember going to bed that night and thinking about the talk we were planning the next day and I remember thinking to myself that I had been doing too much talking and maybe it was time I let Mark do the talking and I do the listening. I knew there wasn't anything that I could say to him tomorrow that I hadn't said a thousand times before. Maybe after I heard what he had to say I would know which direction it was that we needed to take. I don't remember if we had the talk we had talked about so I am assuming that we didn't because our lives just continued status quo.

A few weeks later I remember Mark was leaving again for work and as he was leaving he asked me if I thought we could end this and be easy on the kids. I remember I had this feeling of strength. I didn't know how long it would last but I said "fine." I told him he had given me his decision and yes I would work everything out for him. I don't know where I got the strength to say that but it came from somewhere. Now I just had to hope and pray that I didn't completely fall apart like I had the last time I no longer had him in my life.

I knew this wasn't going to be an easy road and inside I knew I still loved him. I remember lying in bed alone that night and thinking to myself, fifteen years. How do you even begin to say good-bye to fifteen years? I watched a slide show that I had made for Mark which was our story.

I remember wishing he would watch it before he left so that he would take some of the good memories with him and not just the bad. I still loved him with my very soul and I wasn't too sure what to do about that. I guess there really wasn't anything I could do. I just needed time to face what I was going to do about all of this and where I was to even start.

I remember thinking about how we couldn't continue on the path that we were on but I also knew that I didn't want him to go, so I left him a note on his pillow the next morning when he got home and I went for a drive. When I came home he was out working on something in the garage. I asked him what he was doing and he said he was fixing something so I went in the house. I remember being upset because he hadn't mentioned the note and was just acting like everything was normal so I went back outside and I asked him if he read my note. He said "ya." I said "well, did you understand what I was trying to say and how I feel?" He said "I guess so." I felt like I was having a one way conversation. I remember saying to him "given the situation we are in right now do you really feel that it is appropriate to just say to me that you are staying out here to fix something?" Things just went from bad to worse at this point and he just started to blame me for everything again. I remember asking him if there was anything in our relationship that he didn't see as my fault. He eventually said no and that it was all pretty much my doing. I asked him if there was just one thing in my relationship that wasn't my doing and he said "well I think there was a car accident a few months ago", referring to the one Penny had been in, and he said "oh ya and there was an earthquake somewhere else I think." I couldn't believe what he was saying. Eventually I saw that we were getting nowhere and I went back into the house.

At this point I remember feeling like there was nothing left to fight for. I was so upset and I didn't know what I was going to do. He came back into the house after an hour or so and he didn't mention the conversation and neither did I.

I was starting to notice the effect the lack of communication between Mark and I and the constant fighting was having on my boys. They loved him as dad, he had been there since they were three and five years old and they were now young teenagers. There was one day that my youngest said he was going out for a drive because he just couldn't stand the fighting and he needed time to think and to be alone. I imagine they were so torn and I knew at that point that something had to be done I just didn't know what.

Again time seemed to just pass with neither of us willing to take that final step, I guess because we both knew that we still loved each other, we had just lost our way.

I remember when Kerri, one of our foster kids who had lived with us for about three years went with Mark to work. There were nights when Mark would take one of the kids with him in the truck as he was only ever away from home for about twelve to fifteen hours and it was exciting for the kids and company for Mark. I was sitting out on my back deck drinking my morning tea and just thinking about life when Kerri came out to sit with me. I had asked Mark what they had talked about for so many hours and he would just give me a short glib answer like "oh nothing important just cars and stuff", but there was something in his eyes that just set off alarms in my stomach and I knew he was again lying to me. I think he does that a lot. I am just now starting to pay attention.

The morning Kerri came out to join me for tea she started talking to me about her trip with Mark and she told me that he had a conversation with her about Lana. She said she thought it was odd that he would bring her up in conversation. He kept referring to her as "the girl." He told Kerri how his mother had gone into Lana's workplace and that she had told Lana that she could understand why Mark was with Lana because she was the type he always looked for.

I was very hurt that he was still thinking about her after so much time and I was also concerned and hurt that he would discuss this with our foster daughter. Why had it even come up in conversation and what else was discussed that I didn't know about if he would go as far as to confide this to Kerri? I was left wondering what Mark had told Kerri about Lana and how he felt about her, but I knew that was information that neither party was going to disclose to me. What hurts the most is that he lies to me and with a straight face and has no remorse for having done so.

I remember talking to Mark a few days later and asking him again what he and Kerri had talked about so I said "Mark I want to ask you something and I want you to answer me quietly because I don't want the kids to overhear our conversation." He looked at me with obvious anger on his face and he said to me "I don't know, what did we talk about?" I told him what she had told me and he gave me his usual line when he doesn't want to admit to something, he said "I don't remember talking about that, it was obviously more important to her and to you than it was to me." I had no desire to go another round with him so I just got sad and said "ok" and I left the room. I didn't say much for the rest of the night until he came into bed. I told him how my gut just couldn't let go of this feeling that he was lying to me and that this was not a conversation that you would forget having, you either did or you didn't. He said he might have said something about it and that maybe they talked about her. I said "maybe, you don't remember talking about Lana or our relationship but you remember talking about cars?" He got angry and started raising his voice to me so I said "if you're just going to yell at me then you can just stop right there. I can't handle that right now." I didn't know what I was going to or what was going to happen to us but I just dropped the conversation again with no resolution or peace.

I didn't really know at this point what I wanted to do. I just knew that at this point I didn't feel very good about him. I could see that he was lying to me and I was growing very tired of his hurtful words and his lack of compassion or empathy. I could plainly see his inability to accept responsibility for his behaviour. Why couldn't he see how all of this made me feel and how he had so let me down? I didn't know how to get past all of it. I just knew that I couldn't continue to do what he was doing and that was to act like everything was ok and nothing had even happened. I had been doing that for so long now. He just always seemed to feel that he never had any making up to do or apologies to make. Again this made it very hard to forgive and move on and to feel loved or respected.

In the following few months' things seemed to continue in the same routine. We got sidetracked temporarily as Kerri was moving out and going off to college and we had to get her set up in residency and my oldest was leaving home as well. So I guess our problems kind of got put on the back burner which for a short time felt like a relief or a reprieve.

I did a lot of thinking, actually it seemed to be all that I did and I finally had the big talk with Mark about what I was thinking and feeling. I told him how I felt and what I wanted and needed from my relationship. I told him I loved him with all of my heart and soul and that I wasn't trying to hurt him or give him ultimatums but that I just didn't have faith in him and that his word didn't mean anything to me at that point because he never kept it. I told him that I didn't trust him and that I didn't feel safe with him. I told him the different ways that he had been treating me that was inappropriate. I never raised my voice or argued. I just talked to him.

He tried a few times to get defensive and to turn things around but I just refused to let him get me off topic or to engage in the fighting. We had done far too much of that already. I told him that he had the right to make choices just as I did and that if he didn't feel he could give me what I needed he could tell me and move on. If he wasn't willing to do what he needed to do to repair the hurt then he should just say so. I told him I had to do what was best for me in order to survive no matter how much it was going to hurt me. He asked me how long until I ended things. I took a deep breath and I told him that if we were still living the way we had been in two months then we needed at that time to sit down and figure out the best way to end our relationship so that the kids were ok and financially both he and I would be ok. At least that way we could be kind to each other. I told him that I hoped with all of my heart that he would do what he needed to do to save us but that I had also gotten wise enough to know that I couldn't fix him and that I could only protect myself. I told him that I still loved him with all of my heart. I hugged him and told him that I would now like to start the rest of our day, cuddle on the couch and watch a movie. I told him that from this moment on I was going to walk forward as our past was killing us. I was no longer willing to argue about the past and that today would be the first day of our healing and that I hoped he felt the same way. He held me really tight and I do believe he really listened to me as we talked and that he had taken me seriously.

That night when we went to bed he talked to me like he really loved me. He held me in his arms and he kissed me for a half an hour and he caressed me for a long time. He even told me that it had been too long since he had kissed me. I went to sleep that night loving him and feeling very content and a little afraid at the same time.

The next day he told me that we should go away for a weekend and that we should start doing all of the things we should have been doing. I started to get scared as I was afraid to have too much hope because this had become a pattern with us. We would have these talks where we just couldn't take any more and then we would both be so good to each other until we got back into a routine and then we would just start to argue with each other all over again.

For some time Mark's behaviour was great. He actually came back from town one day and he held something behind his back. He walked over to me in the kitchen and from behind his back he pulled out one long red rose. He kissed me and he said it was just because. I think I thanked him a hundred times. It made me feel so good, it made me feel like he had been thinking about me when he was out which in turn showed me he cared enough to try to repair us. Maybe there was hope for us yet.

The peace seemed to continue for a few months but eventually things started to go back to the arguing and miscommunication. I remember we went to my niece's Jack and Jill out of town about an hour and a half away. On the way home one of my anxiety attacks hit while we were driving. We stopped at a local gas station on the way home and Mark went in to pay. I didn't think too much about the night as nothing seemed out of the ordinary.

It was a few weeks after that Mark just kind of slipped some information into a conversation we were having about how a previous friend of his Greg and his wife Heidi had separated. He hadn't had any contact with these friends for at least twelve to fourteen years so I found it odd that he would have any knowledge of their marital status. I asked him how he had come upon this information and that I found it very odd that she would just randomly come up in conversation. He told me that he had seen her at the gas station where she was working some time ago. I asked him why he had not told me when he saw her and he said "you were in the car, you were laying down I think having a panic attack and I didn't think it was a good time". I asked him when this was and he said a long time ago. So I said "so that was almost a year ago?" and he said "ya, about that." Again I had that old familiar feeling that he was lying to me.

The next day Wayne called me at home and said that he was going to tell me something that I probably didn't want to hear. He told me that he had been talking to Heidi and that she had told him that Mark had stopped in where she worked the Sunday just previous and that he had asked her for her phone number. I couldn't even believe what I was hearing. It hurt and yet at the same time it felt just all too familiar. I was so angry. I remember confronting Mark on the two-way while he was at work to see if he would be honest with me. Once again that didn't' happen. I asked him when the last time he spoke to Heidi was and he said "I don't know, why are you asking? I told you before that it was when we were coming back from your nieces Jack and Jill." I said "so it was last year?" He said "ya." I said "so you didn't talk to her at work on Sunday?" and after a few minutes of silence he said "well ya I guess I did." I remember saying "what did you talk about and why didn't you tell me when you got back in the car?" He said he just said hi and that she told him that she and her husband had separated and that was about it and that he didn't think with the day we were having that it was the time. So I said "does that include asking her for her phone number?" He paused and then he said "I didn't ask her for her number." I said "well I happen to know for a fact that you did so why don't you try being honest with me for a change instead of lying to me again." He got quiet for a few minutes and then he started making up excuses as to why he asked for her number.

I knew in my heart why he got the number, I know him. He asked for her number because he knew he and I were probably not going to make it and he had always found her attractive and I believe he figured since we were over why shouldn't he get the number and he would have someone to turn to when we finally took that final step. His excuses for getting her number were no more than that excuses and at best they were very superficial and really not worth mentioning since they were very far from the truth. At this point when he knew I wasn't buying his story he just quit talking to me on the two-way.

When he got home we continued to fight about it. He kept trying to turn the tables and blame me for his lying to me and for once I just didn't buy it. I had finally had enough when he said to me that he knew he never should have moved back in with me when we separated the last time after Lana. He continued on to say that he knew I would never trust him again and that I wasn't capable of letting go of the past, like that made getting another woman's phone number ok and lying about it, so I told him three things. "One, if you call her we're done." "Two, are you willing to call her tonight with me on the other phone and tell her you made a mistake getting her phone number and that your wife wouldn't understand? Will you tell her you love your wife and you won't be calling?" He said "sure." "Number three, if you want me to believe you and trust you then let's start over with a clean slate. Will you give me something to trust? Will you agree to take a lie detector test and tell me that you were only with Lana twice? Was the affair longer than only those two times and have you slept with any other women that I don't know about since Lana? If you have nothing to hide then you will hide nothing right?" He said "fine".

Then after supper he sat on the couch and I walked over to the couch with the cordless in my hand and asked him when he planned on calling and he said any time. So I said "now would be good." He just sat there and watched t.v. so I went back upstairs.

The next day about noon I received a call and when I got off the phone Mark said to me "that sounded pretty official." I said "it was, it was the private investigators office. Apparently they come directly to your house to perform the lie detector test." Well that was right about when he got up and went to the bathroom. I fixed my tea and I told the kids that I was going downstairs because I knew he was going to have something to say about this. He then came downstairs and to make a long story short he refused to take the test which I knew he would do because we both knew he couldn't pass it. This way he at least was sure I would never have proof of his infidelities, but he knew that if he failed the test he would actually have to admit to his straying from our marriage and take responsibility for his choices. He could no longer blame me. I think he thought that if I found out the truth we would be done so if we had to be done anyway he would rather leave and still be able to be the nice guy who was the one treated badly. He said that if I needed a lie detector test to save our marriage then we really didn't have any marriage at all. He told me that I should call the real estate company and arrange to list the house that he was leaving. He got up quietly then and he went upstairs to have a shower.

I came up and I waited in our bedroom and when he came in after his shower I said "so this is what you really want?" and he started to cry and was genuinely upset. I knew at least at that moment that he loved me on some level. I remember feeling panic inside and thinking this is it, he is leaving my life and that our story was really over. I had to face the fact that he was eventually going to be with someone else and that in my mind, I was going to be alone and responsible for everything. I surprised myself when I didn't beg him to stay and I didn't cry. We ended up talking for about two hours. Because we both did still love each other, we believed that we owed it to our love, our history together and to our family to give us one more try, he set up EMDR therapy and we found a school for couples. I wasn't really sure what the outcome would be but I knew we were trying.

After we had seen this couple's therapist twice together and once each individually, we came to the realization that this had just become something else to fight about.

Things between Mark and me for the next few weeks were not very good. Mark's lying was just getting so discouraging and I didn't see how therapy would do us any good when he wasn't willing to be honest and it had been lies that helped to get us to where we were. I just got so tired of his changing around the facts and it just hit me that he wasn't capable of being open and honest and if he couldn't do that then how did we even stand a chance? We discontinued therapy.

Mark and I had always made a point of making sure we went to bed together. Now there seemed to be many nights where we didn't bother and truth be told at this point I preferred it that way. The years of deception had just become too much and I didn't see any end to it in site. My life just seemed to have become nothing but mass confusion and I couldn't see any way out. It just didn't make sense any more. Just when I thought I had figured out where we needed to go from here. I would have a few happy days with Mark and I would start to have a little bit of hope all over again and try to believe that maybe this time everything would turn around for us. That didn't happen.

Chapter Nine

The distance

I find it rather amazing how one day you can perceive your life as being one way and then the next day your perception is completely different. Our lives seemed to go in cycles like this. We would go for periods of time where everything felt like a normal family and a normal marriage and all was calm. Then everything would just fall apart. I couldn't understand how at one point I didn't even want to be around him, where I was haunted with images of his being unfaithful and my fears of who would be the next one. Then when he seemed to love me, was kind to me and cuddly and affectionate I would start to berate myself for having such thoughts at all because it was obvious he loved me. After a while you really start to question your sanity and I'm sure everyone around me was questioning my grasp on reality as well.

It was my daughter-in-law's (that's what I called her), twentieth birthday and I awoke feeling life was good. I got out of bed with a smile and went for a walk. I was happy for the first time in a long time. I felt free, the wind was blowing in my face and the smell of fall was in the air and the temperature was perfect. I was actually dancing when I went around the block listening to the music. Had anyone seen me they would have for sure thought I had lost my mind.

Mark came home from work that day and was visiting with everyone which was nice. He came and told me he was going to have a shower and I had this immediate reaction that just came out of the blue and surprised even me. All I could think of was wow he's getting awfully cleaned up just to go to work and I know it's crazy but every single day Heidi is in my head. I feel like I'm living another Lana, it's just a matter of time. He didn't ask her for her phone number just to not use it.

Today when I couldn't reach him on his two-way in the truck I actually went for a drive in my convertible and I was going to go to the gas station where Heidi worked to see if he was there or if he pulled in on his way home. So when he was getting cleaned up again for work I said something like "wow, you're getting awfully prettied up for someone going to work." When Mark goes out with me he doesn't even care if he brushes his hair or puts on clean clothes. Anyway all that was going through my head was its Saturday night and Heidi isn't working at the factory (which was her day job) tonight. Is she going with him?

He came downstairs and wanted to hug me and he said "Oh I think it's cute you saying how I'm getting done up for work, that's cute." I said "I'm glad you found it funny." He replied with "oh, it's cute." I was so angry. I thought you selfish heartless prick. He wasn't the one dealing with the baggage, I was. I was the one that every single day thought about him and Heidi taking their friendship one step further. After all what was stopping him, he obviously didn't see fidelity as all that important. I just needed answers.

There were so many times where all I wanted was to be close to him, but always in the back of my mind were the conversations that he had with me where he told me he was leaving. He never said anything to me to change that fact and I guess I was constantly waiting for the day he would make it a reality. He had a way of saying hurtful things to me one day and leaving me to my fears and then he would be nice to me the next day but not take back what he had said, so I had no way of knowing which statements from him were the ones he really meant.

One night I was up in bed and Mark came in and knelt on the floor beside me. He put his hand on my breast and looked at me. He said "I miss caressing you." I didn't say anything. I just looked at him. He asked "why doesn't it feel comfortable and natural?" I just looked at him and said "I don't know." He said he tried to kiss me today and he did, he had pulled me down on his knee and was giving me little kisses but I just wanted to get away.

It's not that I didn't want to be close to him that's really all I wanted. It's just that deep in my heart I believed that he would never change and if that was to be the case then I needed to keep myself distanced from him or I would never survive his leaving me. I didn't think I could survive it now let alone if I allowed myself to fall in love all over again. How could two people who from their own perspectives really love each other and get so far off track that communicating became impossible? It was like we were speaking different languages because I don't think either one of us was at all understanding what the other was trying to convey. I think looking back we were both trying to deliver the same message and both failed miserably.

The enlightening moment for me that night was when he got up and went to the door to leave to go to work and I was crying because it just felt like good-bye as it so often did those days to me. I couldn't even talk to my friends about the possibility of his leaving without getting choked up. I really still loved him but I just didn't know if I could live with him and forgive all that he had done to hurt me and the fact that he would brush it off so easily with excuses. I needed acknowledgment from him for what he had done.

We watched a movie that night about a couple in love. I wanted to reach out and touch his hair that night but something stopped me. In the movie, the couple danced around in the living room in their underwear, they kissed and laughed on the street and they couldn't stop the passion between them. I wanted that. I used to have that. What happened? Now I just felt shy and inadequate with my own husband. I wanted to be carefree and safe to just be goofy and do crazy things with him but I was afraid he would correct me or criticize me or just plain ask me what I thought I was doing.

I never get to feel like he is just mine. I always feel like he is mine and hers, whoever her may be at this given moment. I couldn't understand loving him like I did, how I was supposed to let him go and know that someone else would be lying in his arms. We were not supposed to ever end. We were supposed to be forever, I was sure of it at the beginning. How was I supposed to just let go?

On Thanksgiving night Mark and I spent it fighting for about five hours straight. I remember thinking what kind of mother gives her kids this kind of Thanksgiving. Mostly what we were fighting about was Heidi, Mark's lying to me and how I didn't trust him but the part that hurt me the most and actively broke off another little piece of my heart was when Mark came to bed, he left his underwear on. Now that would probably sound like a stupid thing to be hurt by except that

Mark and I had always slept naked. So when he climbed into bed I said "sleeping with our clothes on now are we?" to which he replied "well you said when we are not getting along you can't be cuddly and huggy with me and when I go to bed naked and cuddle you I didn't want you to feel any expectations so I thought I'd wear my underwear and that way you'd know nothing is expected of you." I couldn't even believe what I was hearing.

I was so unbelievably hurt and I believe that was his intent. I thought to myself arguing is one thing but with couples to me there are just some lines you know you shouldn't cross because you are going to hurt the other person and cause damage you may not be able to repair. He was obviously willing to cross that line. So I laid there for a few minutes absorbing what I had just heard him say. I was so angry and so hurt at the same time. I got back out of bed and put on my pj's and got back into bed. He said "what are you doing?" So I replied "putting on pajamas." He said "what did you do that for?" I said "because I feel really naked lying here beside you." He said "but you hate sleeping in clothes." I said "I'll get used to it." We both just stayed on our own sides of the bed and I silently cried on mine. My nose got very stuffy so I went to the bathroom to blow it and came back to bed. He said to me "are you alright?" I said "I'm fine." He said "you don't sound fine" and he turned me over to lay on my back and he actually asked me what was wrong. I'm still trying to get my tears under control at this point and trying to talk at the same time and I said "I guess I just feel there are some lines couples don't cross and some when they get crossed just hurt more than others" and I said "but you just want to play games." He said "I'm not playing games." I said "no you're just trying to deliver a very hurtful message and the message has been received" and I turned over still crying. He put his chin on my shoulder and said "this isn't what I wanted, it's what I got, but I didn't ask for this."

It seemed like no matter what we tried we just couldn't seem to stop the momentum but I was also afraid of that last good-bye and not having him in my life. I was afraid that if he left I would find out I really did still love him and it would be too late.

Some things that happen in life are nothing short of ironic. Mark and I went through a three day period where he wasn't speaking to me. I couldn't figure out what I had done to deserve this treatment and why he seemed so angry with me. After three days of silence I had finally had enough. I told him that if he was going to give me the silent treatment I at least deserved to know why. He told me that a co-worker told him that he had seen my car parked outside of a friend of mine's house. This friend's name is Shawn. Mark believed at one time that I had an interest in Shawn that wasn't platonic. This was not the case. I did find Shawn attractive but as it has always been, my heart was with my husband. Apparently this co-worker gave my husband the impression that he thought I was fooling around with Shawn.

I had gone to Shawn's house because one of our foster boys had died in a tragic four wheeler accident and Shawn was the funeral director. I asked him if he could get a copy of a letter I had written to the boys' mother as I didn't have an address for her and I wanted to request a copy of the DVD that had played at the funeral. I had asked Mark many times over to speak with the boys' mother as he was an old friend of hers. He promised he would but it just never seemed to happen and speaking with Shawn was the only other way I knew of to get the letter to her and to obtain a copy of the DVD. I showed Mark a copy of the letter that I had delivered as it was on my computer.

One thing that made me angry aside from the fact that I had been ignored for three days was the fact that my car being there had even hit the radar screen of Mark's co-worker. The only reason that would be the case would be that he and Mark had discussed Shawn before. I thought it rather ironic that he would treat me so badly because of his suspicions and the word of someone he worked with, without even the consideration to ask if this was the case, especially given his past behaviour, ironic.

As time moved on Mark stopped coming directly home from his runs and he would sleep on the road. He would tell me he was tired. I had been with him for fifteen years and he had always come home to sleep with me when he could. It became very obvious he was avoiding coming home. Just one step closer to his leaving.

We had so much to argue about it seemed and we had even started arguing about the money.

Things seemed to be at an all-time low just before Christmas about November. We had a couple of drinks of wine one night and I was ready for bed. I said to Mark "if you're going to fall asleep you should come to bed." And he gave me a rather odd look and said "that's ok I can sleep anywhere." I said "do you want to sleep there?" He gave me a rude look and just covered up with the blanket and went to sleep. We didn't seem to talk much in or out of bed anymore. We hadn't had sex in a long time and I wasn't sure we would again the way things seemed to be going. It had now become uncomfortable to even say good-bye when he was leaving for work. I guess that is how it goes when couples are slowly letting go. I just felt like I had nothing left to say and it was obvious he felt the same way.

Mark and I had always confided in each other when we were going anywhere, we both thought it was just the right thing to do. I remember one day Mark was angry with me and he just stood up and said he was going to the wreckers to get new tires for his jeep and he left. This was very odd for Mark because we always did these things together. When he came back home he told me that he had went to the local car dealer and test driven a new mustang, then went to the wreckers and then he went and cut off all of his gorgeous long hair.

Now this may not seem out of the ordinary for a lot of couples but as for Mark and I it was. Firstly, he always said if he was single he would buy a mustang and he knew I loved his long hair. He had never in fifteen years gone and cut his hair without us talking about it. He was sending me a clear message and one he very much meant to send. He was telling me he was now going to do whatever he wanted when he wanted. I got the message.

I told him that when I looked at the pictures I have of him on my dresser now I see the man in my heart, the man that I love but when I look at him now and I look in his eyes I can't find that person. The man I look at now and who looks back at me is like a stranger and how sad that made me. I was so tired of his indifference. I told him if I was angry at him and was waiting for him to fix things he never did. He just said to me" now why would you do that, it hasn't gotten you anywhere before." He was just so mean by now. I told him that if he couldn't go to work that night and walk back into our home and start treating me with some kind of respect and a little kindness then he needed to leave and go to his mothers.

I didn't want him to leave and have nowhere to go so I told him that come January he needed to leave and maybe he should start looking into where he planned on going now, that his days of abusing me were over. My how you can get buried in anger and because of the pent up anger and resentment you really can't see things clearly at all. Hurt can distort the simplest of facts.

It was December and Christmas was drawing close. Over the month it was like Mark was just keeping the peace with me but he had totally detached from us. It was like we were two people who were so intimately familiar with each other but now we didn't know each other at all, living in the same house and sharing a bedroom. We hadn't been intimate with each other since September and the saddest part was that he didn't even seem to care. We went to bed and he would just go right to sleep while I would lay there for hours going over memories that we had made together.

I was so lonely I couldn't stand it. I was tired of being sad and I wanted to feel loved and desired and cherished for who I was. Was this what all marriages turned into? I was so afraid of ending up all alone and yet I was alone already.

I sat one night in the dark in the living room watching the lights on the tree and the presents beneath. I couldn't help but wonder if this was to be our last Christmas together. I thought about our intimacy and I wondered if the last time we were intimate with each other was our last time.

New Years was on the way soon and the kids were having a party at the house. He knew the heavy bass music generally brought on one of my panic attacks and that I couldn't stay at the party but I was adamant that I didn't want the kid's plans to change so I had arranged for a motel room at a local resort. Mark decided he would stay and party with the kids so I knew that I faced New Years alone in a motel room with a fireplace and one very big bed.

That brought back memories of the previous New Years Eve when the kids were having their party. I had gone up to my room to get away from the loud bass and made sure I came back down close to midnight. When I came back down to spend the countdown with Mark he stayed in the middle of the room with the two young girls my son had invited to the party. He brought in the New Year with them and then walked over to me and said Happy New Years. I asked him if he could leave the music turned down a bit and that way I could stay down there with him. He walked back over to the stereo and turned the music back up and said to me "you should probably just go back upstairs." I remember being so hurt I just went and put on my boots and went for a drive alone. I drove around for about an hour crying and feeling more alone and unloved than I ever had. When I came back home he was sitting upstairs on the floor talking with the same two young girls and he said I shouldn't have left and that he turned the music down right after I did but in the same breath he tore out my heart when he told me that he hadn't even noticed when I left. What would this New Years hold for me?

I knew when he walked out that door that I was going to hurt like never before. I would never dance with him again, I would never feel his arms around me, I would never hear those words from him "I love you." I didn't know who I was without him. He was the other half of me and had been for half of my life. I knew I still loved him even after all we had been through but I also knew I couldn't fix it alone. I thought he was my safe forever. Is there really even such a thing?

We continued to argue through December and decided that he would stay through Christmas and New Years and then he would leave.

When I tucked him into bed one night he asked me why I was so aloof. I told him I had done enough talking for a lifetime and that if he had anything to say feel free because I was always left wondering and never knowing what he was feeling or what he wanted. He said "I told you my thoughts have never changed or wavered. I would stay with you until the bitter end." I told him I didn't want someone to stay with me until the bitter end that I wanted someone to love me and want me. So he got angry once again and asked if the anger was better. I told him I no longer had the energy or nerves to fight with him again that day.

A few days later we found ourselves alone in the house which didn't happen very often. We had fixed a cup of coffee and were sitting at the table when he looked at me and asked when I thought we should separate. We spent most of the rest of the day crying and talking and then crying some more. Neither of us wanted to leave the other, we both still very much loved each other yet we also knew in our hearts that living together was not working. It's funny actually because he talked about asking me out for dinner and if in two years my health was no better and if I realized that it was not him making me sick would I take him back. I told him he would have moved on by then and wouldn't want me back. I was so scared. We cuddled on the couch for a while and I cried in his arms and he cried in mine. I still loved him so much. Was I doing the right thing? What if I wasn't? That night he cuddled me and we watched a movie and when we went to bed we held each other so tightly.

I remember thinking to myself why couldn't it be this way all the time? But I guess in reality it was like we were getting in every little memory we could before we lost it all. Then came the part where you get to talk about who takes what, all the things you achieved together came down to who had what in the end. As crazy as it may sound I was very desperately hoping deep down inside that the separation as hard as it was going to be was the right thing for us to do. I was hoping that with a little space to heal that maybe, just maybe, this would be the start on the road back to each other.

I just hoped he really was my forever.

Well it was New Years Eve and there I sat in my motel room, alone. I remember thinking what did I want most in my life at that very moment. I wanted romance. I wanted someone to come in there and look at me with desire in their eyes and I would want them in return. I wanted him to lean me back on the couch and kiss me tenderly and slowly. I wanted to feel his hands touch my body. I wanted to feel wanted and I wanted to feel desired. Who was I trying to fool? I didn't want just anybody to make all of these wishes come true. What I wanted more than anything under the sun was for Mark to surprise me and come walking through that door, tell me he loved me too much to ever let me go and fulfill every fantasy I had about what love was really supposed to be. But really, how many times had I wished the same wish. Wishes don't come true.

January 8th, a day that will forever be etched in my heart. There we stood at the back door crying. It took about an hour to say good-bye but it was really happening. I just couldn't stop crying and it broke my heart to see my youngest son hug him and say "you're still my dad." God had I done the right thing? Before he left I had to run to the bathroom and throw up. I cried for a few hours, then just pondered my decision. I felt ok with what we had done, that was until I woke up the next morning and it really hit me. He was gone. I cried some more. Then I wrote him a letter and left it on his jeep. He came by and plowed the driveway for me and when he came in he held out his arms and held me and I cried some more. I told him how I thought we needed to do this but that my dream had still not changed. I still wanted it to be him that I was lying beside when I turned 70 but that I wanted us to be best friends and we needed to start over to do that. I told him that I still loved him heart and soul. I told him when he was holding me to please tell me that I wasn't losing him forever. He said no. He did say he thought about bringing me a flower today but he thought I would think it was stupid. Oh how I wished he had. He also said he would call me that night. All I wanted to say to him when he called was please get in you jeep and come home and hold me. I need you.

I ended up getting in my car that night and driving to town to see where he was and I found his Jeep at Duane's house. Duane was a mutual friend and someone Mark had known since his school days. Mark came over the next night and he stayed for supper and after supper cuddled me on the couch as we used to do and we started talking. He was fine with the talk as long as it was my flaws that were pointed out. I listened and said ok I'll work on that. He ended up falling asleep on the couch. When I got up around 1:00 a.m. he was still sleeping on the couch. I woke him up and asked him if he wanted to come to bed where it was warm. He said yes and he just stayed.

As first I felt relief because the pain in my heart was gone. A couple of weeks after he came home I went online to pay some bills and transfer some money from our line of credit to our visa and the bank wouldn't allow me to do it. I reached him on the two-way and asked him if there was a hold on our accounts. I knew Mark had ben to the bank to set up a new checking account because we had separated and his pay cheque was automatically deposited but we had agreed to leave the line of credit as it was until the house sold. I asked what he had done at the bank and after playing dumb for a few minutes he told me he had made it so neither of us could do anything without the other. I couldn't believe it even after I told him I would pay everything and he could take the visa I wouldn't use it. How could he think I would do anything so underhanded as to run up the line of credit? I asked him if this applied to all of our accounts as well as the credit cards and he said just the line of credit. I asked him why he did it and he came up with this, "I wanted you to be sure I wasn't going to run out and buy a car like you thought I would and vice versa." I asked him if he really thought I couldn't be trusted. He said he thought he did a good thing so I asked him if that was the case why hadn't he told me about it. He said "I was going to." I felt betrayed and couldn't help but see the similarities from our first separation.

About two weeks later I was talking to a mutual friend of ours, Duane, and some of the things he told me was nothing short of shocking. He told me that Mark thought I was having an affair with Shawn. He told me that Mark had been checking the numbers on my cell phone and looking them up in the phone book or 411 and can't find them. I can't believe after everything I have been through with him and forgiven him for he is searching through my stuff like he is. He so used to criticize my first husband for the same thing.

Duane told me that he thought that Mark had definitely not been faithful to his first wife and that he wasn't being faithful to me either. He also believed that by what Mark had told him that Mark wanted his independence and his freedom. He said that Mark told him he missed that life. He said he felt cooped up in his marriage. He said that he loved me but that he wanted more out of his life. He said that he thought Mark wanted to go out and play with women but that he wanted to know that I was waiting in the wings when he was done. He said he believed that Mark was looking for someone to play with and that he was getting his little black book ready. Again what came to my mind was his getting Heidi's telephone number and keeping it a secret. Flashbacks from our first separation and his little black book tortured my mind. He told me that Mark had said that he had a real problem with the way that I had handled the money during our marriage.

Apparently, Mark told Duane that I only went out and spent money on myself and the kids and that he got nothing. I was really starting to believe he would leave me eventually if this was how he really felt. It may not be this year or next year, it may be when I turn 50 or perhaps 60 but in time he was sure to leave. I believed there was still a small part of him that thought he still wanted me but it was a very small part.

It was hard to accept that Mark would say such hurtful things about our life together and hearing these things wasn't easy. I couldn't understand how it could not be true. Duane was long-time friend to Mark so why would he lie?

I wondered would I ever wake up and smile again. Would I ever laugh again? Would I ever feel like I had a purpose again?

Mark had just purchased a new laptop and he was setting up his facebook account. He was having trouble logging in so I took the laptop to see what the problem was. The first thing I saw was that Heidi had accepted his friend request. Heidi again. I gave him back his computer and I said "here you go and you can tell Heidi your wife said hello" and I went to my room. I was so full of anger. He had just set up his facebook account and one of the first people he added was her and I was to believe there was no intent or interest there. Did he really think I wouldn't react to that given the history of his obtaining her phone number? He had given me his word that he wouldn't contact her. It felt like he didn't care at all how he hurt me. Maybe that was his intent.

When I asked him what he was doing adding her he actually said to me and thought I would believe it "I didn't know I did." He said he had just copied from my list and I very quickly advised him the Heidi was not on my list. Then he went to his usual excuse "I don't remember adding her." Then the truth came out. He knew that he had added her and he didn't think I should make such a big deal out of it. I couldn't believe he just didn't get it. I was just waiting for him and Heidi to have contact with each other and that would be that.

He continued to add friends to his facebook account that he knew had caused us such grief in the past. Women that had been so openly cruel and hurtful to me seemed to be the first people he added. At this point we had divided all of our finances and Mark was contributing five hundred dollars a month toward joint bills.

On Valentine's Day he shocked me. He asked me out to dinner. At first I didn't know whether to say yes or no because I thought, why now? We are separating. This is just going to make things harder. I couldn't remember the last time HE had asked me to do anything. I used to request that he take me on dates, but it never seemed to materialize. I agreed to go to dinner and wished with all my heart it would have been a beginning for us. He surprised me before dinner with a dozen roses of assorted colors. I was so touched. He had been cuddly and considerate and I was worried about this being just him really trying and it would be good for a while and then he would go back to who he has been.

When we went to bed that night we were talking and I told him I had been noticing changes in him. He honestly didn't know what I meant. He just said he wasn't so angry. When I pointed out what changes I had been seeing, he said he was glad but he hadn't noticed. This was music to my ears because that means it is not a conscious effort that will go away in a week and that maybe EMDR is actually starting to show some positive effects.

Mark and I had a very wonderful two weeks but it was short-lived. One day I awoke and was just feeling at odds. That intuition thing again. I was sweeping the kitchen and I just had the feeling that something was not right, that Mark and I are very disconnected and I couldn't figure out why. When he went to bed that night I checked his facebook and found a very sexual conversation between Mark and Jessica who was a twenty-one year old friend of my sons. She said something about being fucking freezing and he said she couldn't do both. He said he wished he could help her with that but he was scared. He also said "I'll bet you'd look good doing it."

When I confronted him with it he said first it was a joke, a phrase I was getting very used to hearing when he got caught misbehaving. Then he said he was just trying to make her feel better about herself as she was a big girl. I knew in my heart neither was true. He continued on in the conversation to ask her for her telephone number and said he would call her later it would be easier. He had no defense to that he just changed the direction of the conversation. I knew he was doing what he always did and that was to get the need he has in himself filled. That need where he has to know if he wanted to sleep with her he could.

Anyway we fought and it ended with him signing a lease for an apartment. I remember sitting on our couch and he said "so do I need to get an apartment?" I said do you see that the conversation that you had with Jessica was so inappropriate?" he said "no I don't". The last words from me were "then you need to get an apartment." He did.

Chapter Ten

The Initial Leaving

Mark made his arrangements to move out and I just knew that this was something that I just could not be there for. I made arrangements to spend two nights at a motel nearby. That was a bad two days.

Then I thought we had a huge breakthrough. He talked to me one night and he was in tears. He talked to me about the fight we had some months ago, the one where I told him he had to move out. He had told me I was a bad parent because I was at the bar with a girlfriend fifteen years ago and my kids were at home with my mom and dad whom they adored. My youngest, Doug, had a nightmare and Mark came to the bar to get me. He finally told me that his anger at me and his lashing out at me had nothing really to do with me. He told me that he saw his mother and he was the young boy only this time he was big enough to do something about it. He said he hadn't even realized it until he went to his most recent EMDR therapy session. Then we spent about two hours talking about our relationship and how I needed absolute honesty at all times from him whether it hurt or not if we were to get anywhere. We covered a lot of ground or so I thought.

We came to an understanding about Jessica and that conversation and he admitted he had that conversation not as a joke or to make her feel better but as a way of filling a need in him to know someone would still want him. I told him he wasn't perfect and that I expected him to have set-backs in therapy but if he would only try to be completely honest with me and when he could tell me himself then we could start to take baby steps to building trust. He seemed so open to it.

It wasn't long after that when I was looking at his facebook that I noticed a reply from Jessica. Obviously it was a response to something he had sent her. I asked him if he emailed her and of course he said no until he knew that I knew and then he admitted it. Same old same old. So much for baby steps and starting to try honesty. The only conclusion I could come to is he is biding his time until he is out of here and in his heart and his mind he wants it over for good. He also forgot to mention that in her reply to him she said she would honour his wishes and not contact him until he was in his own place. What does that tell you?

Mark went to work the next day and of course he came home late again and went directly to bed. When he got up I asked him if he wanted me to find someplace to be on his night off as he was obviously avoiding being home with me. He just said something mean and went and had his shower. I remember sitting on the floor by my end table and crying. He got out of the shower and said to me "what's wrong with you?" I said "I'm fine." He said "You don't look fine" and he left the room and went to the kitchen and laughed with the kids. He came back in to the room and walked up where I was sitting and he started really raising his voice to me and he said "Janet, you put this relationship on the table. You knew this was going to happen and it has and I'm going to do this and I'm prepared to do this. I don't think you prepared yourself for this and you're not ready to deal with it. Well maybe I'm harsh but I've done this before and I'm going to do it again. Get it together and grow up. We are separating. We are not the first couple on the planet to ever separate so deal with it. It's a second marriage for god's sake we've got a 90% failure rate for fucks sake." He was so mean.

The next day when he came home and he was going to bed he asked me why I was so distant. I said to him "I can't keep saying good-bye to you every day" and he said "do you want me gone?" I said I just can't keep saying good-bye. He got mad and said "you want me gone, I'm gone." I said "you're only here now because you have to be." He got really angry and said "I don't have to be here. I'm gone." He went to work while I cried another hour or so.

The more I thought about how hurtful he had been the angrier and the more hurt I got. When he came home he acted as if he were someone else. He was so nice as if nothing bad had taken place. I told him I was going to town and he followed me downstairs and he asked if I wanted him to go with me. I was in total shock. Was I completely nuts? Did he not remember anything he has said to me? I thought he was coming home to move out and he wanted to know if I wanted him to come with me. More than anything I did but I couldn't do it. I couldn't let him hurt me that way again so I said "no thank you, you pretty much told me where I stand last night." He said "never mind." I said Mark you ripped my head off and tore out my heart last night, you were so mean to me, I didn't know you had that kind of meanness in you." He said "forget it then" and I left. He had also told me when he got home from work that day "you look nice today ma, but then you always look nice." What was he trying to do?

When he went to work I was lost without him. I didn't understand why this was because I had been living the life of him working nights for fifteen years but all of a sudden it was like every time he left he left for good. I remember one weekend he went on a three day trip trucking. He called me while he was away which was good news for me because it meant he was thinking about me while he was gone. He said he would be home tomorrow. I had only one more of each week day left with him and then he really would be gone and I would be without him, maybe for good. How was I going to cope? Would he even miss me and be sad or would he be relieved to be free?

Why did I have to love him so much still? This week was going to be so hard, our last week together. How did I want it to go? I decided to make it about family and fun if I could. We needed something good to end it on or would that just make it harder on me when our last day got there? I just kept thinking well he is still here for seven more days. When will he start to behave like he is single? When will he take off his wedding ring? When will I know it is over?

The next day was uneventful in the beginning. When Mark was leaving for work he asked me to shut down his computer for him. When I went to do this I checked his facebook and that is when I saw his emails back and forth with Heidi. I couldn't believe what I was seeing although I don't even know why it would surprise me by now. He had promised me twice over the last three months that he would have nothing to do with her. I asked him about it and all he said was "oh ya, didn't do it to hurt your feelings." I said I couldn't be a part of his life if these women were in it. His response was "I'll be out of your life tomorrow." It was nice to know he would walk away from any hope of us for women he said he cared nothing about at least that was my perspective at the time.

As much as this hurt, I was sure of one thing. It was going to get worse before it got better. Then came the night before he was to move out. I walked him to the back door as he left for work and he said to me "so you're not going to be here tomorrow?" I said "no." He came over and gave me a hug and I said could you hold me really tight for a minute and he wrapped his arms around me. I cried and I said "we're never going to be together again are we?" He said "I don't know." I said "you're not coming back to me ever, I can feel it in my heart." He kissed me good-bye and he left. I sat at the end of the bar and I cried and I cried. That night was so sad. The next morning I knew I had to keep busy until my room at the motel was ready. I remember going to the liquor store and picking up a mickey of rye and a small travel bottle of crown royal and a can of diet coke and I drove around crying and drinking.

When my room was ready I unpacked everything and I cried a lot. Wayne called and I cried some more and couldn't talk. I told him I was going to have a nap and I'd talk to him later. Shortly thereafter I heard a knock at my door and it was Wayne. He had driven there immediately to see me before he went to work. He left and I was feeling so alone. My youngest son Doug and his girlfriend Faith brought me my son's computer so I could talk to friends on msn. I wasn't too bad while they were there but when I knew they were leaving I couldn't stop crying so I told them to leave and I would be ok.

I was wondering if Mark had ever really loved me. Had I made a huge mistake and I asked Faith to talk to him. I guess she did but it didn't go well. Mark was pretty angry. He was very hurt that Doug hadn't helped him move out. I tried later to explain that Doug couldn't deal with the fact that Mark was moving out. To Doug he was dad, the only dad he ever remembered and he couldn't face him leaving. I tried to remind him of the night when we originally thought he was leaving and Doug hugged him at the door and said "you're still my dad." But Mark was having none of it.

I asked Doug and Faith to have Mark call me. I absolutely had to hear his voice. He was angry when he called and he felt it was me that put us where we were. He said that I asked too much of him by needing to know who he was talking to and where he was. He felt that I was controlling and manipulative. He said I needed to trust him and he knows I can't. He said that I mothered him and that I controlled him. He doesn't seem to feel I have any reason to be insecure. He basically just wanted me to leave him alone but said that in a few days when he wasn't so angry anymore he might decide that he misses me and needs me or he might decide he loves me but that the quiet was nice and he can never go back. I believed he was done with us. Mark told me that our relationship troubles had become who we were and it had become our lives and I didn't really see that until this point. I had to find a way to break my addiction to him.

This is the part of my life where everything changed for me. Before we separated everything seemed to be about past hurts and new hurts and who was right or wrong. All of a sudden with this pain in my heart none of that seemed to matter. I wondered what I had done. Why did I ever think I would be ok without him? Now a lot of women would be totally ok in my situation but I knew myself better than this. I just didn't care about anything anymore.

I wrote this book about infidelity but it is important to understand that there is always more to the problem than just a cheater. There are belief systems, childhood scars and just the differences in character. I didn't realize this until I was already there. So I think it is important that you the reader are given an accurate account of the whole story and in that way you will be able to understand my choices and my decisions.

I had reached an all-time low. I wasn't adjusting at all. All that seemed to matter to me was getting him back and as strange as it sounds I didn't care what he had done I was willing to take all the blame for everything I just knew we couldn't be done. I knew I didn't want to spend the rest of my life without him. This is a tough position to be in given my belief system on being faithful.

I don't know how many of you out there will understand this, but I guess I started to think that even with the fighting it was really important to me to know I wasn't alone, that I belonged to someone.

Crazy in this day and age I know but it is the truth of my world. I just felt so lonely and I felt a sad I never knew I could feel and yet I also felt a sense of dejavu, I had been here before but I had forgotten the intensity of the emotion. I knew deep inside that in spite of all that had happened and for the life of me I didn't know why but I really loved this man for better or worse so for now the only thing I could think about was how to fix us. Everything else came second, I would work on the broken heart and the betrayal later.

We weren't separated for more than two weeks and late one afternoon I just couldn't cope, I felt panic and desperation and I thought the only thing that would make any of it better would be to see him. Maybe I could convince him to give us one more try and if I couldn't I guess as sad as it sounds, at that very moment, I had given up. I really didn't care what happened to me. If someone asked me fifteen years before this moment if a man would ever have this kind of hold on my heart the answer would have been quick to come and would have been a very adamant no way. I would never have thought that love could hurt so badly and put someone in a place where you really can't think logically.

On this afternoon I drove over to Mark's apartment. Before going there I went for a drive and of course played all the sad songs about break ups that I could find, like that was going to make things any better. I drank two coolers and I took two 50mg Demerol and a 1 mg lorazapam. I felt like I was in some bad romantic movie. I actually cried so much when I was there. He was just angry and rightly so that I would have a drink and Demerol and drive there. He doesn't understand weakness and he couldn't understand why I had asked him to leave and then would show up at his apartment in this condition begging him to come home. Frankly, neither did I but that is exactly what I was doing. I told him I didn't want to live without him in my life. By the end of the afternoon I wasn't feeling too well and he had to go to work so I laid down in his bed to sleep and he left. By the time he left he had agreed to us talking and spending some time together but honestly I think it was guilt induced.

Mark came over to the house for dinner the next night and he showed up with a dozen roses and after dinner he cuddled me on my bed for about a half hour before he had to go to work. He told me he loved me and how he didn't like lying down at night alone without my body pressed up behind his. When he left for work I felt my first ray of sunshine as pathetic as that is.

The next night Mark and I went out to the show and then we went back to his apartment to watch a movie. He was there but he wasn't. There was that distance back again it was like a tangible thing between us. All night I was torn between so wanting to be there and knowing that he really didn't want me there. Eventually I left crying and wondering where things went from hopeful to falling apart. He knew that I was upset when I was leaving and I was sitting at his door putting my shoes on and he never came over to hold me or tell me it would be ok. He just sat on his couch until it was time for me to walk out the door and then he just hugged me quick and said good-night and closed his door.

When I left his apartment I was a wreck. I knew I was in no condition to go home and let the kids see me like this so I went for a drive to listen to music and to clear my head. It was like I was driving but not really seeing or caring where I was going. I guess I just wanted to be somewhere that had safe memories for me when everything was simple and happy. About an hour later I ended up in the subdivision where I grew up and sat across the street from the house that for so long was home to me. I guess I just needed to be where I once felt safe.

The next night my sister talked to Mark on the phone and he pretty much gave her the impression that I should try to heal and move on with my life because he was moving on with his. After a lot of crying and sobbing I agreed that I would leave him alone and let him miss me and I would work on getting over him. I went for a walk that day in the rain for about six or seven kilometers and I cried some more. Well I made it until that night and I just had to hear his voice. I beeped him on the two way when I knew he would be in the transport and I asked him if I had interpreted his conversation with my sister the right way and that was that he wanted us to be done. He said he would come by the house and talk to me.

When Mark came by the house I begged him to lean on me and give us a chance. He said he had no faith in us. I told him to trust in me one more time and slowly his faith would start to grow. He said he would think about it but that it wasn't something he could give me an answer to that day. He left and I sobbed some more. It seemed to be all that I was capable of doing those days. How had I been reduced to this person and how could one woman be so weak, and yet I was. It was like I just walked around with this huge pain in my heart.

My sister was really there for me and I don't think I would have made it through had it not been for her. She told me each day I would notice a small change. I was so hoping that I had the strength to leave him alone. So far I hadn't but it was a new day. Mark told me that he does his crying alone that he sometimes holds my picture and cries. I was so hoping that at those moments he would turn to me because he needed a connection to me but he never did which could only leave me with the impression that he was healing and to me that wasn't a good thing at all.

Well it was my birthday weekend and I won't go through the day to day events that got us where we were at this point in time but Mark and I spent my birthday weekend together. I again started to have hope that maybe we were turning a corner and he would come back to me in time.

That Monday I went to town for a walk with my son Ryan and we ran into Mark while we were walking. I was surprised when he offered to walk with us for a while. While we were walking he took my hand which even though it was a small gesture made my heart sore. Here he was out in public holding my hand and in my mind that had to mean something. When he said good-night to me that night he told me that he loved me with a smile. I asked him to call me that night to say good-night and he asked me what time. I said I don't care as long as I get to hear your voice before I go to sleep. He said ok ma (which is what he called me) I will, again with a smile. Ryan said to him "jeeze Mark, you're even starting to give me some hope here." Mark again smiled and said "Rome wasn't built in a day." I went home that night thinking things were going great.

Two days later we met at the real estate office and Mark told me to keep trying to sell the house and he again told me we were over. He told me that he loved me but he didn't want to take this path anymore. He reminded me that when the anger went away so did the love. That his feelings had changed and he was sorry. I felt like I had been hit with a bus. I was shocked. I thought things had been going so well and then out of the blue we were over again. Once again I seemed to do nothing but cry. How much hurt could one person take before they gave up and just dealt with it but no I kept going back for more. I didn't know what else to do.

The next day I called him again and I asked him if he meant it when he said we were over and he said I was doing it again that I was looking for answers. I asked him if he was pulling back because things were going too fast. Then he started to tell me all the things he was angry about when we were living together.

He told me that he was going to continue going to his EMDR therapy and that he would come find me. I told him I loved him and that I would let him go. I asked him to let me hear it one more time before I hung up the phone and he said "I love you ma". I said good-bye hubby. My sister and my friends were telling me that I needed to accept the fact that he wasn't coming back to me and that I couldn't keep waiting for him when he wasn't giving me any hope. All I could think about was that to me he was my every thought, my every feeling and how could I just not feel what I was feeling. I didn't know how to get through those moments when I felt such a driving need to hear his voice.

I remember lying in bed at night and holding the two way close to me and thinking about how if I just pushed one button I could hear his voice and eventually I gave in and beeped him. He heard me crying and he told me that he would come by the house and he did and we talked for about forty-five minutes. I asked him if he missed us and he cried and said every day. It is funny how someone can have an entire conversation and they will take one small sentence from that conversation and that seems to be all they hear. That is what I did too often.

I actually used to think that if I tried hard enough he would forgive me for the way that I had hurt him. It is amazing how you forget everything that was done to you that got you to the point of feeling that you had no option but to end the marriage but when you start actually living that reality and realize you made a mistake you wish you had worked harder to forgive and be more kind.

When you get to this point you somehow become willing to change whatever you are told made the other person unhappy. There was a point where Mark told me that he was very angry over the spending he felt I had done during our marriage. So I immediately went home and sold the hot tub and put an ad in the paper to sell my convertible. I thought perhaps if I sold things to pay down more of the bills that maybe he would see that I was being responsible and that I really got how he felt. Most of our purchases were joint purchases but that didn't matter all that mattered was the Mark remembered it differently so I set out to fix that. It was a start.

Perhaps someone will relate to some of those weak moments when you have a broken heart. There were times when I wanted to hear his voice so badly that when I knew there was no one home I would call his house so I could hear his answering machine. Is that sad or what? I know I know but I'm being honest here I did that. I was getting advice from everyone but the problem with that is that the advice was conflicting. Some people were saying to leave him alone and if he missed me he would come to me and others were saying call him now and again and send the occasional email to remind him that I loved him. I just kept going back and forth. I started to think maybe I should buy a house in a city nearby and start moving forward because living in the house we shared if he was never coming back was just too hard. It was filled with too many memories.

About two weeks later Mark came by the house to visit. We spent about two hours talking and he seemed to be in a different place. By the time he left he decided he would like to see me but he would like to go slow. He told me that he would call me to talk on the phone and that he would quit giving up and when he left I felt the first ray of hope I had felt in quite some time. I thought here I go again.

I remember one night he came by for dinner and he told me that he was getting a nose job done. He had always hated his nose as he had broken it numerous times. I think this stood out for me because of the way he brought the subject up. We had always made our decisions mutually and this time he just blatantly informed me of his intentions. It was almost like he was proving a point. Mark told me that he wanted me every time he saw me but that when he wasn't with me he could control it. He told me that he wanted us and the only reason he wouldn't try again and wouldn't let me in was that he was afraid. He didn't have faith that I would love him forever and that if he came home to that I would never let him go again.

Why couldn't I get to a point where if he decided to come home great but if he didn't then I was happy with me and I would build a life of my own that was good for me? It really felt like something that was so beyond my reach. At this point trying to keep his love was killing me slowly. I needed to find a way to take all the energy that I was putting into trying to convince him to come back to me and put that into trying to find a way to build some kind of an existence that I would be at least ok in. I needed to start facing reality. I needed to find some way to find some pride and to let him go. I couldn't believe that I had reached a point in my life where I was begging someone to love me. I didn't think I was capable of such sad behaviour. I couldn't understand why I couldn't get angry at him and why I couldn't seem to stop loving him. I still don't have the answer to either one of those questions.

So I took that first step I went and got a part-time job at a call centre. I didn't know how I was going to focus on work I just knew I had to and that it would be good for me. The next thing I did was make an appointment to have my tarot cards read to see if he was going to come back to me. Yes I even involved the supernatural. The result of the reading was that I needed to leave him alone or I would lose him forever and that he could not accept the love that I was offering at this time and that patience was crucial. She also told me that I needed to take my own journey at this time because I was going to be a woman alone for quite some time but if I leave him alone he would come back to me. I know in a logical sense this was totally illogical but it did give me some hope that in time we would find our way back to each other.

I was getting to a point where I was getting very angry with his need for total control over how much contact he would permit. He got to choose when we saw each other and for how long, how long he would talk to me on the two way and if the conversation didn't go the way he wanted it to he would very bluntly tell me "don't make me shut this phone off on you." I was starting to feel like a small child in training and I was certainly experiencing my own time outs. I didn't know what to do with all the anger I was feeling but I also knew I couldn't express it to him because that would just push him farther away so I guess I kept that all bottled inside. I was losing a lot of weight, weight I couldn't afford to lose and I was so depressed.

We were spending some time together but he very much was giving me the impression that he was only looking to be friends. There was one night that Mark and I and the kids decided to go to the show. When the show was over our foster daughter Penny said she wanted a picture with Mark so I took it for them. Then she said she wanted one of he and I so I went to stand beside him and he leaned against the wall away from me so I just stood about a foot away from him and she took the picture. I was both embarrassed and hurt at the same time. It was getting harder and harder to spend time with him. In my heart it really was all that I wanted but in reality it just hurt more to be with him and feel his coldness. I didn't want to feel this way anymore but couldn't see how that was going to change any time soon.

He was always playing hot cold hot cold. I never knew whether to give up or keep trying. One day he was just wanting to be my friend and the next he was affectionate. Just when I had decided to give him his space and leave him alone, I went to town with Penny and we were driving around when Mark beeped me on the two way. He asked me what I was doing and when I said just driving around killing time. He said "well you could come hang out at the apartment if you want." I said "is that what you would like?" and he said "I wouldn't have asked you if I didn't." So I went and he was so attentive. He grabbed my hand in his kitchen and walked me to his bedroom and we laid in his bed and talked. He told me it was the birthday cake that made him so distant the night before. Mark has an issue with sugar and it affects his moods. He was holding my hand and playing with my shirt while he talked to me. He said he loved me and that he always loved me and that that has not changed. I told him that he needs to start communicating with me what he is feeling. I asked him why he held himself so far away from me and he sounded so vulnerable when he said "I am trying to err on the side of caution, I wish I had your faith that things would stay this way," but he didn't have the anger he had so often of late. I asked him if he just wanted to be my friend forever and that if he did it would be kinder to me if he would just leave my life. His response was "no I don't want to just be your friend forever, I love you." I said "ok, do you ever see yourself coming home?" He said if we could get along for an extended period of time there was nowhere else he would rather be. So once again I had a little hope.

Chapter Eleven

My Bottom

Just when I thought I had discovered what sad really meant my sister talked to Mark on the phone and he told her that his relationship with me was over, that he didn't want it anymore and that he only loves me as a friend, that his devotion to me is gone. He told her that from the beginning he always felt like there was something wrong with the relationship and that he had brought his friend Wayne with him five times when we first started dating to break up with me but didn't do it.

That was the bottom for me. I didn't think I would make it through the night. My sister got me to write him a good-bye email which I don't think he ever read. It was the hardest week of my life so far. It wasn't a couple of days after that I saw that he had added Lana to his friend's list on facebook. I asked him why he did this given our history with her and his response to me was "I'm not asking your permission." That hurt and I thought even for him this was low and hurtful. I found out the next day that Mark had gone to see a lawyer and he was having some papers drawn up.

Part of me wants so badly to believe he will find his way back to me and part of me thinks that it is stupid to even hope for because he said he didn't want me anymore and a part of me wonders why I would ever want him back. The answer: because in spite of all of this I still loved him. Who can say why you love someone or what makes the feelings go away, all I knew was that for me it was still there and I had to believe there was a reason for this.

People told me in a month I would feel better than I did right at that moment. I didn't feel like I would ever feel any better again. I thought maybe the day would arrive where I wouldn't drive by his apartment to see if he was home, wouldn't check his facebook on a daily basis and I would eventually take that step to disconnect the two way on my phone as the only reason I had it was to talk to him. Maybe I would get to the point where I would have a day go by where I wouldn't think about him or I wouldn't cry at all.

Well I was on day four, and day one to four were absolutely horrible and I cried constantly. My Dr. actually sent me to talk to a crisis counselor it was that bad. On day five I felt like crying but I didn't sob. On day six it was hard but I decided to go out and get a little black kitten. I felt like I was breaking the rules as we were unable to have pets when I was with Mark as he was allergic to them. I was unable to get attached to the kitten as every time I looked at the kitten I was reminded of what it represented. So I returned the kitten to the pet store.

I was scheduled to start my part-time job the next day and to start my moving forward it was slow going but I was doing it. I had managed to go an entire two weeks with no contact and for me that was a huge step forward. When I went to collect the mail that day I was faced with mail addressed to Mark.

I thought it was time I tried seeing him face to face to see how I would do. So I went to his apartment and I gave him his mail and I asked him that since we were through what did he want me to do with his mail in the future and which lawyer should I be communicating through. He said there was no papers coming. He lied to me about not having visited a lawyer's office so I was reminded again about his inability to tell the truth when it suited his needs. He started to cry which completely shocked me and he asked me "do you have any idea what it is like to have people come up to me and tell me about how I never loved you. I spent half my life with you. I didn't have kids because I wanted you." I said "well thank you for that, at least now I can know that during our seventeen years together I was loved for some of it." I left after about forty minutes of talking and let's just say I wasn't ready to see him in person. It was too soon. It was like starting all over again at square one. When I left his apartment that night I told him that I loved him and that my heart still was and always would be his.

It was about this time I noticed he had registered on two dating sites and that he had added two young blondes (which was always his preference) to his friend's list on facebook. All I could think was that I shouldn't be surprised at his pursuing women after all he did that while we were together so why not now?

About a week later I received more mail for him and I emailed him to let him know it was there for him. I was very surprised when he emailed me back and in his email he said that he loves me and when he sees me he wants to touch me and that nothing would make him happier than to be with me. It was like we kept going in circles we loved each other but he would run hot and cold and it was on again off again with him.

This made it very difficult to ever stay the course of leaving him alone and it was impossible to move on for me because when he showed me any interest I was again lost. My boys were having a hard time watching me suffer the on again off again. They were rather angry when they heard he had said these things to me and gave me hope again. They told me I was being foolish to think he was sincere and that he wouldn't allow things between us to change and that he was just going to rip my heart out all over again.

I knew they were right but I just couldn't seem to stop myself where he was concerned. It was like I had this sad need to be walked on and hurt. At least that is what it must have looked like from the outside in. I'm sure a lot of you are wondering where my sense of self pride went, my willpower, my ability to be ok as a mother and a woman on my own. I wondered this myself more than once.

He talked to me later that week and he told me that he thinks about sex with me quite often and he has no problem spending time with me but what if he spends time with me and he sleeps with me and it never evolves into anything more than that for the rest of our lives and people will think he was an asshole because he used me. I didn't know what to think of that logic but I did know it would rip my heart out each time he left.

We spent a fair amount of time together the next week and I started to hope that maybe he would be ready to recommit by Christmas and we could have a family Christmas. One night when we had plans for me to go and visit him, after we had sex and we were cuddled together on the couch watching a movie he told me he had a shower before I was to get there and he was washing his hair and shaving and getting all excited because a beautiful woman was coming to see him and then he remembered our situation and said what kind of pathetic loser was he.

It wasn't long after that when I took his hand to hold it close to me while we cuddled and he just pulled away from me and said "just be normal ok, just be normal." I immediately shut down. I just wanted to cry and I didn't understand the change in him. I said "ok" and I just got quiet to watch the movie and he said "don't get weird with that ok?" I said "ok". About ten minutes later he went to his kitchen to make toast and I got up and got dressed. He said "putting your stuff back on are you?" I said "ya." He said "something I said?" I lied and said "no it's just chilly in here" and I sat back on the couch kind of close but away from him. After about half an hour he moved so I could lay beside him but the mood never got back to my feeling wanted there. Before I went home we were at his door to say good-night and he was really mad at me. I couldn't understand what I had done wrong or why he was so angry but he was yelling at me because of my low weight and my wanting to cuddle him.

Once again I thought we had just had a great night and here he was doing all he could do to destroy it before I left. This was a period I referred to as our transition period. He couldn't commit to all or nothing so I had no idea where I stood. He did delete himself from the two dating sites. I couldn't believe it had only been seven months when it felt like seven years.

Mark had what looked to me to be a pretty comfortable lifestyle where whenever he wanted to have sex with me I was there. He had supper at his mother's every night and he had a new friend that lived in his building. She was blonde of course and a stripper and much younger than him. She seemed to come and go as she pleased and he seemed quite taken with her. I knew there was nothing serious between them but he seemed so happy to have her around.

We had plans to spend that Saturday together and I was so looking forward to it. I called him Friday night to see if our plans were still on. I was shocked at his answer. He said "well it's not something I want to do but I don't have anything else to do and it seems pretty important to you so if it is something you really want to do I'll do it but I will be doing it for you not for me." He then went on to tell me that he loved me but that he wasn't in love with me and that he was never coming back to me and that we were over forever. Before he hung up the phone I asked him what he wanted me to do when I saw him on the street. He said "you walk up to me and take my hand and kiss me on the cheek and walk away and that way I will know that our seventeen years together meant something." He told me that he knew we were over because I'm not the one he wants to call when he comes home and I'm not the one he wants to see. He said he can be mean and hurtful to me and he really doesn't care. That was so hard to hear. So when I hear all of this why was I crying all day and why would I ever want him back.

So again I started day one of not contacting him and trying to accept he was no longer interested in being with me ever. It was Thanksgiving weekend and I made a nice roast beef dinner. It was quiet as our house was these days but I made it a nice dinner. At the end of the dinner I went into the bathroom and I sat on the floor and I sobbed for about ten minutes because I missed him so much. Then I came out and cleaned up the table.

I made it about a week and at one point I missed him so much I had to hear his voice. I called him and he was friendly. I told him the truth that I was just calling to hear his voice. He chuckled and said "that's cute ma and it's ok." I told him I was trying to get better at it. I hung up the phone and continued on with trying to stay away.

The next time we talked I was getting worried that soon he would replace me because men don't go without sex and I didn't know if either of us crossed that line that there would ever be any going back. I told him that we had been faithful since we were married (or so I thought) and that this was still at least ours. I told him that I wanted us to still to only sleep with each other until we were 100% sure. He said he didn't know if that was such a good idea because he didn't know where it would lead or that I would be able to handle only seeing him for sex. I didn't know either but it was a way to get to hold him sometimes. I guess my life had reached a point of waiting for the phone to ring. It didn't.

I knew I needed to re-establish the belief inside of me that I am worth something. I do count even without him in my life. He did not define me it was just easier to let him. I needed to start having faith in myself and find some things I enjoyed even though I didn't quite know what that was going to be. I deserved to be happy and I deserved to be loved and not have to bargain and beg for it. I needed to let myself feel the grief and to take steps to get through it and I needed to quit making excuses and running back to him every time it hurt. I knew if I continued to do that I would never heal and yet even knowing all of this I didn't know how to make myself do it. It was all just words, my heart wouldn't co-operate.

I will still waking up shaking and feeling sick to my stomach and I had a doctor's appointment that day and I was actually proud of myself because for the first time I didn't drive by his apartment on my way by. It was such a small trivial thing but it was huge for me. I went to bed that night and I got teary eyed a few times but I didn't lose it. I did cry once that night but only for about five minutes. I was giving him what he wanted I was leaving him alone I just wished it didn't have to hurt so badly. I was supposed to take the two way off my cell phone that day but I just wasn't ready to do that yet it was just too big of a step yet. I had reached a point where I was angry and missing him at the same time. I saved my crying times for when I was alone in the house or in my bed at night.

I went to visit our mutual friend, Duane, to talk. While I was there I deleted Mark's number from my cell phone and his truck number from my two way. This was a big step for me because if I had a weak moment and wanted to hear his voice I had no way to reach him because I didn't know the number for his truck. I later talked to my sister on the phone and she told me to think of my life in chapters and we all know each chapter has an ending. So I started to think back over my life. My chapter with my first husband was full of good memories. I didn't regret that chapter even though I knew it had to end. Then my chapter with Mark started. I learned what it felt like to love someone so completely. Now I know what love feels like. I also learned what an unhealthy love is. He helped me raise my boys and he provided well for us. I now needed to accept that this chapter to was over, he no longer loved me. Now I needed to start my new chapter and learn how to move through the heartache and learn to love again. I needed to focus on selling the house and moving somewhere new.

I still had not contacted him and it was over a week. I didn't know what kind of strength I would have if he showed up at my door or called me. I decided I was going to do my absolute best to move forward with my life and to let him go if that was what he wanted and it appeared he did.

I was being asked to go out and have a drink with Shawn but I just didn't have any interest. My friends were calling and were very supportive. When I was talking with some friends I was told that Mark had been seen walking around town almost daily with Heidi and that this was who he had been spending his time with. It felt like someone put a knife right through my heart. I wondered since he got her phone number while still living with me and she is the one he now spends his time with how long until they make it official or I saw them together and what would I do when I did? How was I going to feel when I saw him holding her hand?

The next day out of the blue he called me. He wanted information on a couple that had looked at our house a few weeks ago and here I was hoping he called to talk to me. Our phone call went bad quickly and he said he wasn't going to get into this big long thing with me on the cell phone and that he would call me when he got home if I needed to argue. I was angry and I told him I had no interest in getting into any big long thing with him and that I wasn't going to play his games anymore and I could not allow him to keep hurting me.

I called him later that night as I drove around with a glass of wine. He asked me what I was doing and I told him driving around processing. He asked me what I was processing and I said "you're phone call". He asked me if I wanted to come up to his apartment for a visit. I said "do you want to see me?" He said "sure." I went over and we talked quietly for a while. He said nothing had changed for him but he did tell me that some of the mean things he says to me are because he is trying to push me away because he has given up on his getting his health back and it would be better for me to move on without him. He said he does still love me and he misses me too and that he did have days where he wanted just to hear my voice but he wouldn't allow himself to call. He said he thought about sleeping with me but that he didn't want me to think he was using me but that he couldn't commit to anything. He told me he wasn't having anything to do with anyone else sexually and he didn't plan on it. He told me that even though he didn't know what the future held for us that he did know that if he was to seek out any sexual activity with someone else he knew that he would be tarnishing us and he was afraid of doing that because it would ruin any chance of a future that we might have.

He told me he would go to the bank the next day and try to max out our line of credit to pay me off on the house and that way he would move back in and I could purchase a condo in the City close by. He also asked if I would prepare a separation agreement and I started to see the reason for this requesting my visit. He wanted to seem friendly and giving so that I would agree to his terms on the house. He knew I had worked for a lawyer for years and it would be cheaper for him for me to prepare the documents rather than him pay someone else and here I thought he actually missed me.

I made arrangement to move to the condo on December 15ᵗʰ. The next time we spoke he told me he needed the closing date moved up to the 1ˢᵗ and that Heidi was taking over his lease on his apartment. Well it seemed to me that what my friends had told me was his game plan had finally played out perfectly for him it seemed. He would have his nose job done and paid for by cash, his big screen and huge stereo, the nice furniture, and he got his house back and he had me out of his life. He never had any intention of coming back to me. I didn't want to believe he was capable of being as cruel as he had been with my heart. He told me part of the reason he wanted the house back was in case we ended up back together. I didn't know what to believe at this point.

He asked me to come and visit one day and like my usual self I jumped at the chance. We had sex and he didn't touch me and I felt so used. When we were talking in his kitchen after he asked me if I would draw up a separation agreement. He said the bank needed it to advance funds on the closing of the house deal. I was dumbfounded. How could he have sex with me first and then hit me with this? He was really starting to show me who he really was, so I thought, and that was not a very nice person so why exactly did I cherish the moments I saw him? Why did I let him use me for sex and yet refuse to even add me as a friend on facebook when even Lana was on that list? Why even though he refused to return my emails or phone calls did I keep going back.

Chapter Twelve

Heidi

One of Mark's friend's son was killed in a fight and they were having a benefit dance for him. Mark told me he was going and I asked him if he minded if I went as well and he said he didn't care. He told me he would call me that night but again he never did. I got myself all dressed up and Penny and I went to the dance. After about an hour of being there who walked in the door but Mark and Heidi and her sister. He didn't come to my table to say hello. I was so hurt that he wouldn't take me to the dance and then knowing I was going to be there he showed up with her. The same woman whose phone number he got while still living with me. The same woman he swore he had no interest in. You could tell just by looking at him that he had been drinking for some time. When Mark did come to the table I think it was only to be close to Penny and he did dance slow with me but only on Penny's request. He just treated me like anyone else that was at the party, an acquaintance.

Heidi and her sister made a point of trying to ruin my night. Whenever Penny and I would dance they would make certain they danced right beside us and would bump into us. I felt like I was back in high school. I asked Mark to please speak with them and ask them to kindly leave me alone. He refused and said I was seeing what I wanted to see. When I left Mark was outside and Heidi was trying to get him to go back inside the dance. When we were leaving he saw me coming down the stairs and he gave Penny a hug good-bye and told her not to ignore his emails and that he loved her. I didn't get a hug however he did lean down and kiss me quick and said "I'll call you tomorrow" and he went back inside. He never called.

About a week or so after the dance and my leaving him alone he called me. He asked me if I was driving around bored and I said why. He said he wanted to know if I wanted to come over and have a hot bath with him. I told him that depended. I asked him if I was coming over to have sex and then get kicked out or did he plan on spending time with me. He said "well I am going on yesterday's clock. I'm ok now but once we have sex I'll probably fall asleep." I don't know where I got the strength but I said "well as much as I would love to see you I have to say no because I don't want to be used that way." He said ok and he seemed to understand. There was silence for about 20 seconds and neither one of us hung up the phone then before he did he said "I do love you ma." I said "I love you to hubby." He said I could come over and visit the next night and to come by about 6:30 but he would call to let me know he was home. He didn't call so about 5:30 I called him to confirm 6:30 was ok. He told me he was visiting and I asked who with. He said Cindy the stripper down the hall. He told me she had cooked him dinner. I asked him if 6:30 was still ok and he said "sure" but I could tell he didn't want me there. I asked how he was feeling and his response was "indifferent."

Well the day arrived of my lawyer's appointment to sign the separation agreement. I cried in front of the lawyer while I signed it. It all just seemed so permanent. I saw Mark later that day and he said it was an emotional day for him as well and he was just numb. He did tell me that he was working towards us as best he could and that he did want it to work. Later that night Penny and I went in to

Mark's apartment and visited for about an hour and a half. Well it was more a visit between Mark and Penny. I wondered if I would ever not be jealous of his feelings for her. I just wanted to matter that much to him.

I didn't see him for a few days after that and I was again getting so tired of always being the one to go to him. I found that he had a profile on Plenty of Fish and when I was at his apartment and I looked on his laptop and he had about 25 pictures of Cindy the stripper as well. I was so angry. When I talked to him later that night on the two way I asked him about Plenty of Fish and he said he had made that profile about six months ago. I didn't believe him and he said he would take it down. I think this was on Tuesday and I said "well I'll let you go because if you had wanted to talk to me you would have called so I guess I'll see you on Friday." He said "so does this mean I should stay away until Friday?" I said well you would have anyway wouldn't you?" He said "well actually I had planned on coming by tomorrow to fix an antennae." I said you are welcome to come by any time you like and use the garage. He said "what, you don't want to see me?" I said of course I do but I want you to call me and say hey how is your day did you want to come over? Or I stopped by for no other reason than I wanted to see you not just when you want something or something needs to be fixed." He said "did you ever think maybe I use that as an excuse to see you?" I said "then could you please stop with the excuses and just say you want to see me?"

Well moving day arrived and I got all my belonging moved to my condominium. When the move was all done I came back to our house. It was so empty but all I wanted to do was stay there that night on my own. Have a glass of wine and walk through the house with my memories. I stayed for a while but I was scared and so lonely. So I talked to my son who said "mom come home, we love you, and I'll unlock the door for you." So I went to my new home.

I noticed he was still on Plenty of Fish so I set up a fake profile of a blonde and emailed him to see if he would respond and if he did what would he say. He answered the email and gave me his full name and asked that I add him on facebook. Then he deleted his account.

I found out from a mutual friend that Mark had been visiting a past friend of ours. Her name was Claire. She was an ex friend, petite and very out-going sexually. He had always had an interest in her from the moment they met. Now I found out he was visiting her as well. I had thought this would be one of the women he would pursue because in his mind he was free to do this. During this same period of time he was spending a great deal of time with Heidi. He would take her to dinner and the show and they would hang out at her place or his and have drinks together. They were even seen going for walks at night together. But he still would get angry at me if I asked him anything about Heidi and say she was just a friend. I had this feeling deep inside me that told me they had feelings for each other and that they were seeing each other and keeping it quiet as she was in a relationship at the time.

Then everything changed. I went to Mark's house one night when he was at work and I looked on his computer. What I found shook me to the core. First I found out that the night of the benefit dance he took Heidi home and they fooled around and I found this out by looking at an email he was sending to Kerri to brag about it. He told her that he knew he had to end it with me but that I was finally after a long time giving him sex so the power was nice but that he needed to end it soon. Secondly, I saw a conversation that took place between he and Heidi where they both said they wanted to be in a relationship with each other. She said she had feelings for him but that she didn't want to make a fool of herself if he didn't feel the same way. His response was no that she was taking it exactly right. I felt dizzy, sick, panicked and destroyed all at the same time. I confronted him and he said she had slept with him but that they were both drunk and had just staggered home and spent the night throwing up. He had a two bedroom apartment but I guess he forgot that part and he dismissed the part where he and she said they wanted to be with each other. I told him I could put it behind us but he needed to get rid of her as a friend because they had crossed a line and he said "ok ma if that is what you need". The next day he called me and he ended it with me. That was December 13th. My sister and I went over to his house and I took back the card that I had given him for his picture frame slideshow and I took his laptop and I deleted all of his pictures of me and him and I went on his facebook and deleted his album of our wedding and the album of me entitled my wife. I was so hurt and so angry. I told him if he didn't want me in his life he didn't need reminders of me and with his memory he would forget me in days but that I would not leave him with intimate data of me so he could sit and show Heidi and I'd be their joke. He said "I'm sorry ma I just don't want to do this anymore, I just don't feel the same." I knew why he didn't feel the same way about me, he was to in lust with Heidi, she was new. I left and went home and cried some more.

I had reached a point where I just had no energy, I just laid in my bed and stared at the wall. I was tired all the time. I felt like a stranger to myself.

There was another woman Mark had become friends with. She had gone to school with my oldest son but she was a few years younger than Mark I believe. She also was a blonde and her name was Laurie. After he started spending his time with Heidi, Laurie contacted me and wanted to come to my home for tea. She told me that she had pursued him for some time. She said the first time she spoke with him on the phone she called him about midnight and he talked to her on the phone until 6 a.m. She further told me that he called her just about every day. She said he used to kiss her and tell her he wanted to be with her that she never knew she might just be his third wife. He told her he couldn't have sex with her but they could please each other in other ways. She said nothing happened. I just didn't know who to believe anymore. He told her we were completely over and that he just couldn't get rid of me. What was I doing? Why didn't I hate this man? He lied to me constantly.

I cried for about a week and then one day I took a Smirnoff and went for a drive over to see Mark. I took him back the slideshow of us and the dvds. I said I was sorry for my actions and anger when he ended us. I told him it was not who I was and that I didn't want our last good-bye to be like that. He still said he hadn't had sex with anyone else. He said Heidi slept with him because he was lonely but that she just cuddled him and he said the only reason she was there was because he missed me. I found this so hard to wrap my mind around because if he missed me so much why didn't he take me home after the benefit dance? Even if what he said was partially true, he may have been too drunk for sex and ended up getting sick but the two of them went back to his apartment with that intent. He told me she cuddled up behind him and that she reached over in front of him and rubbed him but they both ended up getting sick. He told me we were 100% done and that he still loved me but he wasn't in love with me any longer. He said he believes we are done but that he wished we weren't. He said he still missed me. He said I will never divorce you. He said "I have only ever married two women and you know I loved Terry and there will always be a soft place in my heart for her. We had a lot do good times. I had to close that door on her. Then I loved you. For some reason you seem to want me although I don't know why so I'm not closing any doors."

I left his house that day with a vow to walk away and finally let him go. I had no other choice he was killing me. I started the new year trying to find something positive in each day even though it was hard. By day seven I was not doing great but I was doing it. I had not contacted him in any way in a week, and I knew one week would become two and so on and so on. On day seven he called me and he used some excuse about wanting some paint chips to match paint. He talked to me like we were best buddies or something. I just couldn't do it, I loved him too much and I knew if I let him keep doing this to me I was going to be sad for the rest of my life. I told him I was moving on without him. I loved him still completely and I did but that I had to try and get my heart back and try to move on. He said "good for me. I will always be grateful for the time you gave me and I will cherish the good". I said "thanks". He said "I love you". I said "I don't believe you anymore". I said "I have to give up the affection from you, the intimacy, my best friend. I have to lose everything and it hurts but I will get thought it. I will be ok". I was crying by this point and said "I will always love you. I have to go". He said "good-bye ma". I said "good-bye Mark". That was it that was all. There was finally an ending to our eighteen year story.

I wondered in my heart why did he have to give up on us. I had so many fears. I had to figure out a lot of things like how did I get my heart back, how did I not love him anymore when he was the other half of me? How was I to get financial security, what was I going to do for a job to ensure that I could pay my bills other than the foster care? How was I ever going to be able to feel even a part of what I felt for him for someone else and how was I to let that first man touch me and not cry because it wasn't him?

Chapter Thirteen

Moving Home

Mark contacted me again in a few days and we talked some more. I knew I should stay away but I had no power to do that. I loved him. We started spending some time together over the next few months and I won't keep writing about the back and forth and the ups and downs I think by now you get the picture of what my life involved at this point. He and Heidi had seemed to have drifted at this point.

Mark agreed he missed me and he said he would let me and the kids move home that summer. The night he told me I could come home was the happiest night of my life or so it felt that night. It wasn't all great during that transition. He would act like he had conceded and let us come home not because he wanted us there and had no doubt but because I had not given up and he was tired of coming up with reasons why we shouldn't try it. A lot of the things he said to me hurt but I got to come home. I just kept telling myself what I had spent a year and half praying for was finally happening and I was going to make us happy if it killed me.

It was a bitter sweet homecoming. I was so happy that Mark and I were reconciling but it felt awkward moving back into the house. I felt like I was living in Mark's house. I felt like I had to ask permission to do anything around the house. This passed quickly though and I started to feel more at home. Mark and I were ok with each other but I could feel in my heart he wasn't yet reinvested. Wonderful, Heidi was still in the picture and I couldn't handle it. I knew in my heart they had shared sexual experiences with each other even though he still denied it. I had found out that there was a night where he had her out to his house and they had drinks together and she again spent the night in his bed. Again he had told me nothing happened. I may have been a fool but there was no way that was true. I knew Mark when he had a few drinks and there is no way she slept in his bed and they did nothing together. What made it harder for me than his spending the night with her in his apartment was the fact that they had spent a night together in what was our home.

So when I moved back home and she was still his friend and emailed him and talked to him on the phone I was haunted by her staying a few nights with him, his email to her and hers to him where they said they wanted a relationship with each other, his getting her phone number while we were still together. All of this was haunting me but I was afraid to say much because our reconciliation was so fresh and I didn't want him to regret it so I suffered inside. I found that now that I wasn't spending all of my energy trying to just hold on to him my ghosts of the things he had said and done during our separation were coming to the forefront. I couldn't seem to get him to understand that given his history with her that there just wasn't room for her in our life. So we fought a lot about her. The emails back and forth, the phone calls. Eventually when she wasn't paying him the money she owed him we finally took her to court. He finally realized she was avoiding paying him and now that he was no longer interested and since he wasn't available for her she ditched him. He finally saw she wasn't his friend. This finally cut their ties with each other and this made things much better between he and I.

There were still issued around trust for me and he was still in the frame of mind that he can flirt with anyone and it's ok. Now I must say I made a lot of promises while we were separated and I meant them at the time, about how he could talk to whoever he wanted to and that I would trust him. I thought maybe knowing all I had been through he would be kind to my heart and not be so flirty with every woman he came into contact with but I was wrong and I had really underestimated the effect it would have on me. I kept it to myself as best I could. After a while I guess I started to rebuild trust a bit because things were going alright. I was starting to trust maybe he loved me.

After being home for a month or so Mark was getting to know Tracey a new foster child at least to him. She was a placement that moved in while we were separated. She was a very pretty girl with red hair and a beautiful face, very petite. He started making a lot of compliments about how beautiful she was and he started calling her a pet name, red. I didn't mind him commenting on how beautiful she was but he would do it every day and I was still trying to rebuild my own self-esteem and believe he found me attractive again because remember he spent a lot of time telling me his feelings had changed and he didn't feel the same way that the love went away. That was all still pretty fresh for me. He would tell her how beautiful she was so often that I started to get angry and one day I said to him "Mark, I get you think she is beautiful but I really don't need to hear it ten times a day." He got angry of course. There was one day she was in my kitchen commenting on how she didn't like her body and she had a kid's body. She was sixteen at the time. Mark's response shocked me and this response came after me numerous times telling him how I was getting really tired of hearing what he thought of her looks when he said how beautiful she was. His response was "oh you have a woman's body, trust me I notice." I was so hurt, angry and shocked all at the same time.

Then the first heartbreak since my moving home happened. I moved home with such good intentions. I was talking to my heart and had convinced myself that he never would have let us move home if he wasn't 100% sure I was what he wanted. Then the day arrived where my heartache was again a new one. I always knew Mark was a womanizer, I had lived it but this one really threw me. I came home from work and I sat on the couch and the other girl, Tina, we had living with us at the time said something about how she thought it was funny about Mark and Tracey that day. I asked what she meant and I asked him what he had said and I could tell he was uncomfortable telling me but I pushed the issue. Finally he said "I thought it was funny, I was lying on the couch and you were at work so I told Tracey to come cuddle me." I asked him for details of how he worded it and he said he told her "oh come on Janet's at work come cuddle me." I just sat there and said nothing. He said "I take it you don't see the humor in it?" I said "no I don't find it funny at all." We had an argument about it because I thought it was so wrong but it was only a comment and I didn't want to get too bent about it.

Penny kept asking me if I thought they had cuddled and I said no he wouldn't do that but she kept pushing and finally I asked her if she knew something I didn't and she said "yes ma, I know that they cuddled on the couch." I couldn't believe what I was hearing. I was so upset I could feel the anxiety in my chest I couldn't even breathe. I confronted Tracey and she said she did it. I confronted Mark and he said "ya." When I asked him what part of his brain could come up with even the smallest part that would make any of this even slightly ok? He said "if you want to make more out of this than there was, go ahead." He said I was taking something that was supposed to be funny and painting a bad picture. I told both of them they could spend zero time alone together. He apologized to Tracey the next morning right away and then went out to the garage still angry with me. I was so hurt and angry that she got an apology and I got anger. I went out to the garage and I said "well I see you fixed the one relationship that matters to you." He got mad and said "well I'm sorry I don't do things on your time schedule." I tried again to get him to understand how this was so wrong to do and that he could be criminally charged. I knew a line had been crossed but I didn't even want to admit it to myself. He got very angry and stood not a foot away from my face and he pointed his finger at me and said "you don't get it do you, I'm not staying long." I was stunned. He did this thing and now he was threatening to leave me. I said "well I guess that makes this disagreement a moot point then" and I cried and said "if you could please just give me some notice as I have to evict my tenants from the condo" and I walked back in the house, ran a bath, lit the candles, started my cd and grabbed a bottle of wine.

I sat in the tub softly crying and let the tears roll silently down my cheeks. I was so sad, so defeated and was thinking I am going to be alone again.

After all the efforts I put into putting this marriage back together to end up like that again. Mark came into the bathroom and he sat on the floor and he leaned against the door. I told him he needed to tell me what his plan was because he not only held his future in his hands he had all the power and held mine to. He proceeded to blame me for Heidi and he told me it was my fault that he had cuddled Tracey because I was too controlling. I couldn't believe what I was hearing. This was no apology he was just driving the knife deeper into my heart like he had been doing the year and a half we were apart. This was the man I had grown so familiar with. I remembered this feeling. I said "well, all I ask is that you let me know when you make your decision because I have plans to make." He was quiet for a few minutes while I still softly cried. Then he got up off the floor, walked over to the tub, leaned down and kissed my lips softly and said "I'm not in a hurry to go anywhere" then he left the bathroom.

The next couple of days went by and then weeks. He never did correct his actions or his threat he just left me emotionally standing in that garage and hearing those words "I'm not staying long." Each day I waited. I became afraid to mention Tracey to him gain. I was afraid to do anything that would make him angry with me or he would leave me. He had me living in fear and I hated being that weak. However, I knew I would not be able to take losing him again. I didn't know how to even start to build trust for him and he was mad that I didn't trust him. I was afraid to go to work and him be home with Tracey because I wouldn't be there to police them. I knew he thought she was beautiful and now he had cuddled her on my couch and he had her body pressed against him. I couldn't get that picture out of my head so I asked Penny to watch them for me. She said she wouldn't let them be alone together so I felt a little better.

My self-esteem was about zero while we were separated, he had been so mean and hurtful. Now he was drawn to a sixteen year old in my home and I just felt like I was nothing. There was no way I could compete with a young girl when I was 47. This took a long time to work through. He wold often say to me when my insecurities came through that I should quit doing this to myself. He would say "I don't have a girlfriend, I'm not doing anything wrong." After a while I learned to deal with it, explain it away and to justify why I should stay. Whereas in reality, I knew I was justifying it because I couldn't leave him again.

There were other things that were hard on my heart. One was his facebook account. He had a photo album on there of his first wife Sarah. I asked him why he had pictures of her on his facebook and he said someone he knew asked what she looked like. I said ok so show them one picture why an entire album. I found it to be very hurtful to my heart each time I saw his album entitled "my first wife." His explanation of why it was there really wasn't believable because he had put every picture of her and the ones of the two of them in this album. He had even made comments on the pictures. He had always worn her as a trophy. When he tells anyone about her he always describes her by saying "oh she was the good looking one, she had blonde hair and blue eyes." I just have always felt like there is still a part of him that is still in love with her and always will be. I will never be as pretty as her in his eyes.

He also had pictures of him and Heidi partying while we were separated which he left on his facebook as well. He also had pictures of him and Laurie as well. There were pictures of Laurie at his apartment the day after he got his nose job done. This was when he told me he wasn't up to company but here was the proof that he was. The part that hurt the most was that he had not one picture of me on his facebook. There was no album for us or me. I mentioned how this hurt me numerous times but nothing changed.

Things were starting to go along pretty well in spite of all the hurtful reminders. I was still trying to do everything right so I would be good enough to keep his interest.

It was about this time that things started to change between Penny and me. We had always been so close and had been through so much together. I didn't understand the turn around. She was spending a lot of time with Mark and at the same time telling me how she didn't think much of him and was getting along with him for me. She told me that she hated him for what he had done with Tracey. She started smoking and we had an argument over her choice to start smoking at eighteen. I told her if she made that decision she was not to get her cigarettes from Mark, we would not supply her habit. I told her not to go to Mark for cigarettes because that would cause fights between he and I. She promised me she would never put me in that position. I also told Mark the same thing. He said he wouldn't give her cigarettes, he promised me.

I then started to notice that whenever he went outside to smoke she was there. I asked him many times to ask me to keep him company that I felt left out because he was pursuing Penny. He would ask me to go out with him if she wasn't home but if she was I didn't exist. Then I noticed every time he went for water in town or anywhere she went with him. She was starting to wear his coat when she went out. It got to the point that when they were talking and I came around she would look at me and say "never mind." It was so obvious. Then whenever I tried to discipline her he would jump to her defence even when she was wrong. He would paint me out the bad guy.

There were so many things I thought nothing of but then it was as if something changed and the dynamics were different. He was acting like he was her husband and I was on the outside.

One day when I was coming back into the house again Mark and Penny were outside having a smoke. I knew that she didn't have any and that she was smoking his. So as I walked by I said "and what are you smoking?" She just looked at me. I knew he had given her cigarettes even after promising me he wouldn't. I came upstairs and I looked on her bed and sure enough laying there on her bed was a brand new pack of cigarettes. I asked him if he gave her the cigarettes and he said no. I said please don't lie to me Mark. He said "no they aren't from me." I was quiet through dinner and went to his car to see how many packs of cigarettes he had left because that was where he kept them and I knew when he bought his last carton. I confronted him later and he confessed and said he wouldn't give her anymore. I went into her room and told her that hurt and that her and I had always had a closer relationship than that and she said Mark gives them to her. I knew there was something going on.

Women have that intuition when something just isn't as it should be especially when it comes to their partners. Mine was screaming I just didn't know what exactly was going on I just knew that something was different between the three of us. All of a sudden it seemed as though it was Mark and Penny and then Janet. How had I been demoted in my own marriage? All I knew was that he was defensive when it came to anyone speaking badly about Penny. They could criticize me and he was ok but he always jumped to her defence the way a husband protects his wife or a wife protects her husband. I wasn't being given that courtesy I was accused of picking at

Penny and seeing things that weren't there and making an issue out of things that were normal teenage behaviour.

Time would answer all my questions and I would come to wish I was still oblivious to the reality of the truth. A truth that would shake my world and change me in a way that I could never return to who I was.

Chapter Fourteen

The Ultimate Betrayal

I remember distinctly when I read those words, the ones that shattered so much of my world. "Mark wanted to experience Penny." I suppose an explanation is necessary.

I took into my home and my family a girl from a troubled past. She was fifteen when she came to me. My heart went out to her immediately and a bond was formed that I thought would last a life time.

Four years went by and memories were made. I had found the daughter I never had and a best friend that I trusted with all that I had. Some people told me not to make her my friend but try as I might to not form that friendship, it happened anyway.

There were so many things we went through while she was growing up. She told me she loved me, that she had finally found the mom she never really had and I believed her heart and soul.

When she was seventeen my husband and I separated for about a year or so and Penny came with me to my new home. Mark and I never really ended things and it was my primary purpose in life at that point to save my marriage and to put my family back together and this included Penny.

The signs were there way back, I saw them and when I did I felt that intuition that said be careful here, something is just not right with this relationship. Mark had always had a soft spot for Penny, I knew that but thought it was a fatherly kind of affection.

I remember how during the separation Mark would send her emails and in these emails he would tell her how much he loved her. He would say things like "you're smile is like the sunshine, it just so brightens my day." There was an email where he told her that he didn't know why he felt the way he did about her just that he did. There were so many years where I asked him to write me letters or buy me a romantic card. These things just never happened. Then to see the loving words I so desperately wanted from him being written for someone else really cut me deeply. There were times when we were being intimate and he would talk about Penny being part of it. I would get very sad inside and hurt that he was thinking of her but I would put it down to men fantasize. I told him it bothered me after a while and he no longer mentioned it.

I remember how he would take her to the movies and even though there were other kids in the home, including my two sons who he had raised since childhood, she was the one that mattered to him. She was the one he pursued spending time with. He told me he missed the kids and that is why he was taking them out. However the others didn't receive any emails just Penny. I put this down to the fact that when we all lived at home he wasn't very close to the others. There was one night at the Condo Penny came to me and said she was uncomfortable with an email Mark had sent her. It simply asked her to send him a picture of her breasts. I said if he is making you uncomfortable you need to tell him to stop and if he continues to talk to you in this manner you will stop all communication. She said she would do this. I don't know if she did or not.

As I think back knowing what I know now so much has changed and so much now stands out so strongly and I am left wondering why didn't I see it back then and do something to stop the flow of events? But I guess that's why they say hind sight is 20/20.

I can remember that new years eve. I lived in my condominium with my kids and Mark was out at our house alone. I knew that I loved him more than life itself maybe that was part of the problem. He used to say I loved him too much, whatever that means. I should have seen so much like when I was told "I wish I loved you like you love me." But wanting us to work so badly, I swallowed the hurt of those words and kept trying to show him we were worth it, don't give up.

We had joint friends and their kids were also friends with Penny. I remember not wanting Mark to spend new years alone. I decided to stay away from the party and asked Penny to invite Mark up to the party for a drink so he would be around people and not by himself. She readily agreed and I was grateful.

I remember her telling me that Mark came up to the party and he seemed to have a good time. I was told she stayed there for the night but that she missed me. The next time I spoke to my husband he said he had an ok time and that he didn't drink much. I thought that was that and didn't put any more thought into it until recently when everything fell apart.

She was my rock during that time and we spent most of our time together. Then the day came when I got the happy news from Mark. He was letting us move back home. I had worked a year and a half towards this goal and it was finally coming to fruition. I thought finally the world makes sense. Here is the fresh start we have been waiting for. No more fighting, I knew where I had gone wrong in the relationship and I was going to make him happy no matter what it took.

I was home about seven months and Penny was now eighteen. Everything was changing and not for the better. She had always had issues with drugs and alcohol and we had managed to keep her on a pretty good path for most of her high school years and she was getting ready to graduate. Well when she turned eighteen it was like someone flicked a switch. She started coming home drunk and stoned after school, she was partying a lot and with the drugs comes the moods. I wouldn't allow this behaviour in my home so we started to argue about it often.

I guess this is where I started to notice the shift in Mark. For that last few months she lived with me she started turning to him to share her sexual stories. She would come home and tell him about her sexual encounters, she would seek him out to keep her company for a smoke outside and when he went out to do errands and I was at work she always seemed to be at his side. Whenever I would talk to him about her behaviour he would always jump to her defence. It seemed no matter what Penny did he would stand behind her. There were times where he defended her so vehemently that I would end up in tears and still he wouldn't shift his position, it was always with her.

I remember on one occasion when I was pointing out how she was playing one against the other and for her it was working he told me "You're just crucifying Penny." I remember how those words hurt and how deeply they went. Here I was looking for my husband to see my point of view, not necessarily to agree with it, but to at least be a little understanding and compassionate but that wasn't to be, he was in her corner all the way. I remember feeling so betrayed.

There came a point where Penny was just running from one party to another and wasn't home too much but when she was it was with Mark she spent her time. I took her to her room one night and tried to talk our way through it like we used to but she pointed out to me how he made her feel right in whatever she did and I was pointed out to her as the bad guy. I didn't want a lot of miscommunication so I asked Mark to join the conversation. He did. However, the turnout was not quite what I had anticipated.

When I told him all of this his response was once again to defend Penny. I had never felt so much like the outsider in my marriage. I was actually in shock as the light started to come on for me. I remember turning to Penny and saying "I think you're a little confused with the situation Penny, you are not his wife and you are not his girlfriend" and the response was one of shock. I remember she looked at him and he looked at her and then simultaneously they both looked at me. At that point I left the room, I was shocked at the energy between them and reeling from doubt that what I was feeling was accurate.

I vividly remember a weekend Penny had spent at a guy's house partying and she was having an argument with Tracey that lived with us at the time over an ex-boyfriend as teens seem to do. Tracey was arguing with Penny on the telephone and I went upstairs to listen to the argument so that I didn't get in the middle of the he said she said when Penny came home. I went to work the next day and when I returned home I found Penny in tears outside.

When Penny came home on Monday and I was at work apparently Mark followed her around the house telling her that the only reason she was home was because he wanted her there. He told her that he was the only one that loved her that I listened in on their phone call and that we all had a bashing Penny night. He told her that I wanted her out of the house and that he made me email her and text her and that she trusted the wrong person when she trusted me and that she shouldn't be loyal to me. He told her that he was the one that loved her. This was not the case and I was very hurt that Mark would do that to me. I confronted him with this and he said no it wasn't that way at all. He was trying to help her and I. Little did I know what he was setting up for himself. I knew she was telling me the truth and he was lying. I knew he cared more for her than he should.

I didn't understand why at the time but it is more clear to me now. He would adamantly disagree with me on this point, but I do believe that he wanted her to turn more to him and if she and I were not getting along that is precisely what would happen and I guess it did in the long run.

Things were tense around the house for the next couple of weeks or so and all seemed to go back to semi-normal but the tension between Penny and I and Mark and I remained. I was still on the outside.

I knew in my heart that Mark was definitely the one in pursuit as I believe he had an interest in her for a few years and I guess as she got older in his mind it became ok as he now saw her as a young woman. Boundaries were blurred and hearts got hurt.

Penny sent me a text one day and told me she was moving in with her boyfriend. I was hurt to say the least and didn't understand it all especially that she would tell me via text. Mark once again did not stand behind me in my position. He said he would still take calls and give her a hug and stuff as long as the hurt wasn't directed at him he was keeping her close.

Then I heard from her dad's girlfriend that Penny said she moved out because she was tired of being the other woman. That same night I saw a post on her facebook saying "I want you to feel me like my step-dad does." I just felt sick to my stomach. Deep inside I wondered if something had happened and I remembered how he had crossed the line with Tracey. Mark was outside and I told him what Penny had been saying and he put his arms out and held me while I cried. He seemed angry that he would be getting accused of something so twisted and denied having had anything to do with her. He said he was done with her and I felt very supported and happy he cared about me. The next day Mark was at work and Penny started to text me and after about two hours of this she said if she told me what she had done I would never forgive her.

Then came the text that changed me in every fibre of my being. I started getting texts from Penny's new boyfriend. He was telling me that something happened between my husband and Penny and she thought I should know. At that moment the bottom fell out of my stomach. I knew that I couldn't turn away and that I had to know what happened but on the other hand I was so afraid of what I was about to hear.

This all started to cross those sexual lines two weeks before Penny's nineteenth birthday. After about an hour of back and forth he finally told me that my husband had gone into the bathroom while Penny was in the shower and that he told her that he wanted to experience her and that it was ok because he loved her. That was the original story I was given. I was told that it was only oral and only once. That she felt obligated. He said that Mark had wanted sex but that Penny had pushed him away.

Now I am not just looking for a way to defend my husband's choices for there is no defense for them but I also want to enlighten people to the fact that Penny was a very promiscuous girl who would brag about her abilities at giving oral sex to men. I used to think that this was a part of her troubled past, a scar. Penny had always stood up to Mark in the past but all of a sudden she felt obligated and couldn't say no. I felt sorry for her and I told her I would get back to her. I started to try to put pieces together and instantly it didn't fit because if she left because this happened and she couldn't deal with it then if this happened before she got her braces on, that meant she stayed almost two months after the incident before she decided to leave and she never left his side during those two months.

Mark was at work at this point so when I finally got to confront him with this news, I asked him what had happened between him and Penny. At first he said "I don't know what you are looking for?" I said I know about the shower and I'd like the truth from you for a change." He asked if he could get back to me and I said sure and I went for a drive and a cry. I fixed a rye and coke and sat at the beach in my car. He came to the beach to talk to me and he asked me if I wanted the short version or the long version. I said give me the long version. He did admit that she had given him oral sex and that it was only once, that is about the only similarities in the two stories.

The second story, his side, is that he did go into the bathroom while she was in the shower and that she was ok with that. He told me that for the last year she had been bragging to him about her skills in the oral sex department and that she used to joke that this would be her parting gift to him when she left for college. Why I wasn't told this the first time she mentioned it to him is still a mystery to me. He told me at one point that she told him to ask me if I would be ok with her doing this to him to which he said he just told her that is a conversation that will not happen.

He said he had to go pee one day and she was in the shower and he did go in while she was in there and that she didn't have a problem with that. I was still trying to figure out what she was doing at home while all the other kids were in school and I was at work. It turned out this was the day that Penny got her braces put on and Mark was taking her to that appointment. I know she had been very open with all of us that she was concerned that she was known for giving great oral sex to guys and she was worried that when she got her braces on she wouldn't be able to do this anymore. He said he was watching porn on his computer one day and she was standing beside him (she had a porn fetish which she was very open about) while he watched a girl deep throat a man and Penny looked at him and said "oh that's no big deal, I can do that." He said "Oh ya tease me." Well long story short he said he walked over to my couch sat down and dropped his jeans. He said she was quite comfortable about the entire thing. He said part way through she stopped and joked about how we had better not have cameras in the house and be taping this and she laughed. He said she gave him oral sex and then they went back to status quo.

Apparently this happened about two months prior to my being informed. Let me tell you once you get news like this you automatically start to go over every encounter you witnessed, every conversation you had with her and him or that you heard them have together.

Penny told me she was so uncomfortable with what happened that she stayed away from home as much as she could. She did stay away a lot however when she was home the two of them seemed closer than ever, inseparable in fact. I was told that the night before she moved out she was going from her room to the bathroom for a shower and was wearing only a towel. Mark was coming downstairs to watch a movie with me and on her way to the bathroom she dropped her towel on the floor so he would see her naked and covered her breasts and smiled as she closed the door.

I guess having found out about the relationship between my husband and Penny I now understood that my intuition wasn't wrong and that I was accurate when I felt like they were the couple and I was the outsider, even though when I broached this subject with Mark I was told I was imagining things and that he didn't have a girlfriend and he wasn't doing anything wrong. I was told these were my ghosts not anyone else's and I needed to get over it.

Once I had all the information I was ever going to get which I still don't believe is all of it but maybe that's just how it goes you always feel there is more that is being hidden. I started asking questions.

I don't know why women feel the need to do this, it is nothing short of self-abuse however I just couldn't seem to stop myself. I felt I had this driving need to know everything right down to the smallest detail. At first my husband seemed to be very understanding of the questions and he said all the right things. I was told that he would spend forever making it up to me, and that he was so sorry he hurt me. He told me a young beautiful girl like her paying attention to him fed his ego. I said "well congratulations because you just destroyed mine." I do believe he was genuine when he was saying these things to me.

When I asked him why he did it he said to him skin is skin and not a big deal and he figured that if I never found out then no foul. No one was going to be hurt. He couldn't have been more WRONG. I asked him how he could risk everything for a half hour of pleasure from her and he said he didn't factor me into it and that he didn't think he was risking anything. I asked him if he understood how wrong what he did was and he said yes it was wrong he trusted her. Reread that sentence again. I made a mistake I trusted her. The feelings that went through me during these conversations I don't even think words have been invented for yet. What about I'm married, what about I love my wife, what about we spent over a year apart and were lucky enough to get another chance, what about this was someone that we raised as a daughter for four years. This was someone that you were so close to. What about I love you too much to ever do that to you. The levels of betrayal here are staggering. How good could someone be that a married man would risk losing everything in his life just for the experience? Oh to have that kind of allure and draw to a man. I wondered what it felt like to be the woman that the man would risk anything for. I wondered does he miss her, does he miss her beauty, her blue eyes and blonde hair, her talent, her youth?

It is amazing how news like this can completely take over your world. It becomes all that you can think about. You keep going over and over the words, seeing the pictures in your head. You can't focus on anything but the betrayal. You question absolutely everything about yourself.

Not only did I lose my new found trust in my marriage and the faith that things had changed but I also lost my daughter and my friend that I trusted and any self-confidence or self-worth that I had which wasn't much considering the begging I did during our separation for him to give us another chance. I started wondering in my heart if the reason that he let us move home had nothing to do with me and everything to do with Penny. Did he let us come back so he could be close to her? In reality I don't believe this is the case but it is a doubt that will stay with me.

I kept wondering how could he do this to me. How could she do this to me? I spent hours just walking down the country road where we lived and just operating on numb. I would cry and cry and then when I thought I didn't have one tear left I would cry some more.

I asked him to be honest with me finally about Heidi as this incident with Penny brought all those lies back for me. He said to me that Heidi had touched him with her hand and he touched her for a while. He said he went down on her he didn't know why he just wanted to but he didn't like it and stopped. He said he touched her breasts and saw her naked. So at that time he was sleeping with me and playing with her and lying to me about it for all this time. Who else was there that I didn't know about?

He killed something deep inside of me when he got sexual with Penny.

I found out on a Friday and when I went to work on Monday I guess the numb wore off and it hit me. I had to leave work about two hours after I arrived I totally fell apart in front of everyone. I felt like because of what I had been told I in society's eyes would have no choice but to leave him but on the other hand I had just spent over a year separated and trying to fix my marriage. While separated I found out a lot about myself and the one thing that is more predominant than the rest is that I am completely so it seems incapable of being independent and on my own. I lost a tremendous amount of weight and I just didn't seem to be able to function without him. This isn't a pretty thing to admit or something that I am proud of but it is what it is. Given what I had found out about myself during this trying time, what was I going to do now? How could I leave when I loved him so much and needed him so much but how could I stay when I found out that he had an affair with the daughter I trusted? I didn't know which way to turn or how to even begin to find a way out of this mess that had become my life.

I felt like I was just their personal joke. I wondered how many times when I wasn't in the room did they exchange a touch or a look or a caress. Did they both wish I would leave the room so they could touch? Did they tell me the truth that it was only oral and only once? Did they go any further? How many nights when I said good-bye to him at the door on his way to work and gave him a hug did he wish it was her? When he was having sex with me did he wish it was her? I remember all the times when he would tell me how beautiful she was and how photogenic she was. What beautiful blue eyes she had and how he liked her blonde hair.

I found out that he had shared everything with her, he had confided in her my secrets, parts of my past that I am ashamed of and that he had also shared with her a private sex video he and I had made just for us. I felt like there wasn't a part of us that was left for me. I felt like he took everything away from me and he gave it so willingly to her. I was told that he would tell her to flash him when he came home at the door and that she had showed him pictures of her naked breasts on her cell phone.

One weekend Tracey and Penny went on the same camping trip with their high school and when Tracey came home she told me Penny had told her a lot of things. She said that Penny told her that Mark had told her he had cheated on me with a lot of people and that he had even been out to see Tracey's mother. She said she was going to send me an email about all of his cheating. I hope the email arrives and yet I am afraid of what I may find out. If there is more how will I ever stay?

I did find out eventually through Penny that apparently Tracey's mother had called our house one day looking for Tracey and she wasn't home so Mark talked to her on the phone and she was having a bad time in her relationship and Mark told Penny he got up from the table and drove to her house to cheer her up. He told Penny that Tracey's mother opened the door in her housecoat and they talked for a bit and that Tracey's mother opened her housecoat and caressed her breasts in front of him. Penny told Tracey she didn't know what happened after that. Another one to wonder about. Why would he do that?

I asked him if he had been to Tracey's mom's house and he said "ya one day when I was in town I stopped by but we just talked". I asked why he never told me and he said there was nothing to tell he didn't think it was important. What a lie, he knew I wouldn't like him visiting another woman without me given our history. Just another woman and another lie to add to the list. I was sure there was more to come.

Then all the demons showed up, maybe some of them will be familiar to you reading this. I remember questioning everything about myself. I'm too old at forty-eight. I can't compete with a nineteen year old beautiful girl. I am a brunette with brown eyes. I can never have blue eyes and be blonde (well I guess I could but trust me it just wouldn't look good) and I certainly can never be nineteen. I remember thinking I'm boring, I'm not as exciting as she is. I'm not as fun. She makes him laugh and he is just down and angry so much of the time he is with me. All of the ghosts from when we were separated came back to haunt me, how long until he left me? Will he leave me for her?

I asked him if he had sex with her and he said no. I don't know if I should believe this or not. I asked him how she finished the job and he said with her hands.

I asked him how long it took, what she did, where they were, was she naked, did he touch her, all the questions to enable me to make that movie that was to play frame by frame in my head for weeks every time I turned around. I couldn't stand in my shower and I would think of her in the shower and him watching. I couldn't look at my couch and I would envision him sitting on it with her giving him oral sex. It was endless. I remember asking him if he touched her and he told me he reached down and caressed her breast.

I remember asking him what he felt for her. His response was "well I had lust for her I'm not going to lie I did have lust". He said he loved her but it was because of time shared not that kind of love. I knew that was untrue it was in his eyes when he spoke about her or to her and it was in his defense of her at every turn and it was in his actions when he sought her company over mine again and again.

I remember thinking great now she even has his lust. There is no way he will ever look at me the same after experiencing her. I felt so betrayed, defeated, old, ugly, fat (by the way I weighed 130 pounds), not good enough, less than her, actually I felt like a total and complete failure as a wife and as a woman and any sexual confidence I had was now completely gone.

I remembered how when we were separated and I would come over and visit him and we would have sex how he would talk then about having Penny join us and do things to him. He was fantasizing about her even then. He always wanted her. He told me she would look up at him with those big blue eyes. I now hate blue eyes with a passion. I remember telling him how it hurt me when he talked about her while having sex with me and he said men fantasize and he didn't see the problem he was just talking. I remember how immediately my passion would die. I knew even though he said nothing it wasn't me he was imagining on top of him. I never thought in a million years he would ever cross that line and make any of it real. I never thought in a million years she would take part in any sexual act with him.

Then I went through horrible thoughts of revenge. I was absolutely amazed at how you can go from loving someone as much as I loved Penny and then in less than a day you can absolutely hate someone with such passion. Now I know there are two people involved in this betrayal. As wrong as it may seem the reality is that it is easier to be mad at the one you are not romantically in love with and feel you can't live without as wrong as that is. I had been down a road somewhat like this one in the past but never to this depth so I knew that I could not trust Mark around women so I guess what devastated me the most was that my complete trust in Penny had been so badly betrayed. That and the fact that I believed he saw her as a child and it was a hard pill to swallow to find out he had turned to her in lust. He didn't see her as his daughter he saw her as a young vibrant sexual young woman. I wanted revenge so badly but on the other hand what could I do. Nothing, absolutely nothing. Oh I prayed that bad things would happen to her, I had thoughts on how I wished she were dead or that something would happen to take that beautiful face away. I imagined the worst things that I never thought I would ever be capable of wishing on another human being.

But if you have ever been through this you will learn that this isn't usually the way these things play out. Which was the case for me, she seemed to just go on with her life, her parties, her life continued as if without interruption. Whereas mine was in a shambles. She just left the carnage behind and went about her day.

I wanted her to hurt the way she had hurt me yet in my heart I loved her. Experiencing something like this certainly does show you a side of yourself that you never even knew existed and one that doesn't make you very proud of yourself. People say forgiveness is so necessary but let me tell you from my perspective I couldn't see any way that I could even find a small amount of forgiveness. I was consumed with so many other emotions.

I am not yet in a place to know what to do with these feelings. Most people say don't give her so much power and forget about her, these obviously are people that have not walked a mile in my shoes. It is not something that you can just put out of your mind and that's the end of it. Every time you hear she is doing great, starting college and things are going in a positive direction for her you feel that anger. How dare she destroy my life and have everything work out so well for her.

I knew in my heart what I believe to be the truth. It is not a truth that will ever be admitted to and one I guess if I'm honest I will never know for sure but you know as well as I do if you have gone through this that intuition is a very powerful thing and it is very seldom wrong. I just truly believe that my husband had lust for this girl, I believe he loved her as a partner and he saw her as his friend. He certainly trusted her enough to do this and to confide all of my intimate confidences with her with no consideration to what he was breaking with me. I believe that if she had wanted him in the sense of a relationship and if she had told him that she loved him that he would not be with me today. I believe he would have left me in a heartbeat if he could have had her. However, she walked away. He tells me this isn't so but I guess I just have to find a way to convince my heart it isn't true.

I just remember the closeness between the two of them for those last few months and how I was so pushed aside. How my husband didn't touch me for two months and I found out later that was the two months after his encounter with Penny. I believe he didn't have desire for me at that point because he was too much in lust with her.

I felt like the more time that went by the more I would crawl inside myself. I didn't talk, I just felt empty. I would feel at other times like I was going to explode. I had no patience for anything at all, the smallest thing would make me so angry I wanted to throw things and then cry. I felt like I was coming apart at the seams. I didn't get any benefit from this. There was no fleeting moment of taboo for me no excitement or physical pleasure or ego boost but I was sure paying a high price. I felt like I was going crazy.

I didn't know how to talk to Mark, I just didn't have anything to say. Every night I went to bed I would dream about Mark and Penny and how he was having an affair with her for a long time and he was in love with her. Every time I woke up and went back to sleep I went right back to the same spot in the dream and I would wake up with tears on my face. I wondered did he have any concept of what this had done to my heart. Did he even care? I find I have so many triggers now. Nothing about our relationship is untainted since Penny.

I remember looking at pictures on my computer one night and I came across a couple of pictures that had been taken by Penny the new years she and Mark went to the party at our friends. Both Penny and Mark told me that they met at the party and that Mark went home not too late. But when I looked at these two pictures which by the way were head shots of the two of them with his face beside hers and you could tell she was holding the camera in front of them. They looked like the happy couple. I noticed that the background was my basement. More lies. Just when I thought I was making progress getting through this mess and I thought maybe he had told me everything I find these pictures. When I questioned him about them he said he didn't remember. Then he said she wasn't at the house then he said well maybe a friend dropped her off he didn't remember. When I talked to the friends that had the party I was told that they thought something just wasn't right about the relationship between Mark and Penny. They said firstly that they both arrived together and late in the evening. They said Mark sat on a chair and Penny sat in his lap with her arms around his neck and that Mark had his arm around her butt. They thought this odd given Penny's age and the fact that they thought Mark was the father figure in her life.

I asked Mark about this as well and he said it never happened. Then he said that she had too much to drink and she came and sat on the edge of his chair and he put his arm around her so she wouldn't fall off. Again it sounds nice but the behaviour was totally wrong. Why did they lie to me about being at the house and I guess now I will forever be haunted by what did they do at the house or did they do anything? He says no.

Mark finally admitted to me that he had feelings for Penny. He also started to open up to me about how he felt during our separation. He told me that he missed me when I was gone and he was very sad. He finally admitted that every time he saw me he got more sad and missed me more so he would avoid seeing me and he said yes he did take people out on dates. He said to try and stay busy and not think about me but he said it didn't work because he didn't want them he missed me. That was nice to hear but I had to wonder would I ever get his heart back from Penny. The fact that he was hurt by her showed me how much he felt for her and the fact that it turned sexual also shows those feelings that he had for her were of an adult nature, he loved her. He didn't use her he shared something emotional with her. I think the word he used was that they had a "mini-relationship."

I remember a night when I thought I was finally getting through the worst of it and I knew, at least my husband told me, that the one thing that I was good at and that gave him great pleasure was oral sex. I know, too much information, but let's face it we aren't talking about card games here we are talking about cheating. I thought, you know what I'm not going to give my power away to her anymore and I was feeling pretty confident. So I took my husband to bed and I started to show him just how good I was. Well let me tell you that certainly backfired. It was like I was on a mission the entire time thinking I'll show him I'm better than her, he'll erase the act of him and her from his heart and replace it with one with me. Well time passed and he really wasn't getting all that aroused. Now we did have sex the night before and I must be honest he has had an issue around arousal for quite some time and we are still looking for answers to that but that is another book. I remember him pulling me up and saying just come here and he wanted us to have sex instead. I felt so foolish, I felt like I put myself out there and I had a plan to erase at least this hurt a little and I couldn't do it. Where I had always been successful I had failed. I remember the tears running silently down my cheeks as I tried to not let him see them. I went to the bathroom to cry a little and wiped my face and came back to bed. He cuddled me and said "what's wrong?" After some prompting I said "I guess it just hurts that she can do that to you and finish you and I can't". Instead of sympathy I got angry words. I believe they were something like "you need to quit doing this to yourself." "Apples and apples if you leave me alone for two months you could do it quickly too but we just had sex last night." I remember just getting quiet and I waited for him to go to sleep.

I remember the entire time I was trying to pleasure him all I was seeing was her doing the same thing. I remember a night where we were being intimate and I started giving him oral sex and he reached down and caressed my breast and my heart went cold. All I could feel was those familiar feelings all over again. This is exactly what he did to Penny. My desire was gone and it was another moment of hiding the tears. Again I was told I was doing it to myself, as if it was a conscious choice. Did he really think I did this for pleasure because let me tell you there is no pleasure in thoughts such as those, there is nothing but devastation and complete sadness.

Just recently there was another attempt to see if I could be successful in pleasuring my husband the way I envision she did. We hadn't been intimate for some time so I thought hey this time it's apples and apples so I took my fragile confidence to bed. Again he didn't seem to get very aroused and he didn't want it for very long before I suggested I could use my hand and he said ok. There I was again, I had failed a second time. My heart plummeted. Has she changed this for us forever? I must say it certainly makes you want to shy away from trying the same thing again, it has forever changed my confidence in that area, in sex in general really.

I now see myself differently when I am naked, I see the age in my skin, I see the extra fifteen pounds, I just want to be dressed or lying flat to look my best. I find it so discouraging that after twenty years of sharing your life with someone when you should be at a point of security and trust that they love you no matter what, I am now more fragile than I have ever been. I have no security that he will love me forever and stay with me as I get old. I feel too old for him now after his encounter with a nineteen year old girl.

This goes on for a very long time. My husband was patient for the first few weeks but after that there were moments when I would look in the closet for something and find a picture of her and I would see that beautiful face and I was right back at that very first moment all over again. I would ask him questions and ask him why he did it because I am a true believer in that if you don't figure out why you did something then you will repeat the behaviour. Well he didn't want to talk about it and got very angry at me. He said he wasn't going to do this for the next twenty years and all of a sudden I was the one who was wrong and in trouble. I said can you promise me this will never happen again and his response was "I can try" and then he said "well as long as we are getting along then there is nothing to worry about". I just looked at him and said "so as long as there is never an argument in our marriage I'm safe". In reality that is no safety at all, to me it was nothing more than a message telling me it was only a matter of time.

I felt so hurt and I cried and yet I was so angry and disgusted at the same time. I thought how could you, how could you do this to me and then have the nerve to yell at me because I feel it. I remember saying to him that it had been four weeks since I had been given the news. I was still here fighting to get through this and I was sorry if it wasn't all wrapped up nice and neat as quickly as he would like it to be but that it was going to take as long as it took and that it was up to him whether or not he wanted to stick around and clean up this mess that he had made.

He did come around and cuddle me and talk to me quietly until the moment of anxiety passed. There are still those days where I feel hey I can get through this and then there are those days where I am so angry and hurt and depressed I feel it will never go away. I don't know when or if that will change, I guess time has the only answer to that one.

It is just really hard to believe that he won't cheat again given his outlook on cheating. He says his father is a runner and his mother was a runner so he comes by it genetically. Well if that is in fact true then where in the hell does that leave me?

Really what am I doing here if it is genetic how is he ever going to change the behaviour long term? What will happen the next time some beautiful blonde girl comes on to him? He admits he has no willpower but says he loves me.

There is more to this story I haven't divulged yet. I provided foster care for teens and had for ten years. I also work in an office three days a week. I always knew that no matter what I could take care of myself financially, I had the income to do that. Well, when news of this behaviour came out to the Children's Aid Society, the teens were removed from my home on fifteen minutes notice and an investigation commenced. It was heartbreaking packing their stuff and walking them to the door. I remember being so sad and yet so angry inside that this was happening. I had always lived my life trying to make the right choices. I didn't do anything wrong, I didn't deserve any of this.

The girls were not returned to my home. I guess I just feel so angry inside that I am the one that has lost so so much. I lost my trust in my husband, the faith that he will be my best friend and the trust that I can tell him anything and know it will stay between us. I lost my daughter and my friend whom I trusted completely. Not only that but I had to lose one of my jobs as well, one I prided myself on and that was being a parent. I lost my financial independence which is a tough realization. I guess I'm angry because I feel like I am the only one that has paid such a high price. Sure he has guilt and shame but he has a wife that has stood by him no matter what, remember the one that loves him too much. He had his experience of Penny so he doesn't have to wonder what it would have been like. It is like he gets that I am hurt and that I am angry but he has no concept of the depth of that hurt and devastation. I think he thought it would be short term and in his mind it's well ok I did this now let's just move on. He doesn't have the hurt heart, the shattered trust, the devastation of who he is as a person. He just seems to go about his day as if all is good, just as she does.

I thought I was handling things ok but I had become very closed off. I didn't talk to Mark much or my kids and at work the other girls would visit and I would stay to myself. I felt so down, defective and hurt.

I was just starting to feel nothing and that scared me. It was almost like I was saying uncle I give up.

I have told him I need him to tell me he is here with me because he loves me, that he is so sorry that he hurt me so deeply. I need to know that he gets how deep this goes. I need him to tell me what he feels for me and why and what he doesn't feel for her. I need him to talk to me on his own not only when he feels under fire and is trying to justify his actions. I have asked him to write me a letter about what he loves and how he feels about me so that when a moment of total anxiety hits and they do, and if he is at work I can go and read his words to me and that this may help the anxiety pass and the love return. I am still waiting for a letter that will never come.

That leaves me with a feeling of how much can he love me if after all that he has done when I tell him what I need him to do to help me through this he doesn't deem it important enough to do.

Now I don't want people to think he is uncompassionate or cold. There have been moments, mostly at the beginning where he would take me in his arms and tell me how very sorry he was that I got hurt. That he never meant to hurt me. He told me how ashamed of himself he was and he actually got choked up. He told me that he didn't deserve my love or devotion but that he was very grateful for it. He told me he couldn't believe that he allowed himself to be seduced by her and that in no way did I deserve any of this. He told me I am beautiful and that I had done nothing wrong that this had nothing to do with me. One thing I can say is I wish it didn't but somehow I feel very involved and given the consequences it has everything to do with me but I do know what he meant by those words.

Well this is going to be a long time healing and I really don't know what the outcome will be. I love him, that I have never doubted and I think I have spent the last twenty years trying to show him just that. I have read all the books that are to help you find a way to heal such as what to do after an affair and books on how to forgive for love and on and on and on but you know what I'm still here in the same emotions trying to find my own way.

There are more days now where I only think about it a few times during the day, it no longer engulfs my entire existence but I feel the healing is only beginning. I find myself sometimes standing on my back deck just quietly looking at the sunset and I'm just unplugged and quiet. I feel just sad, numb, alone and hopeless and then there are days that I spend alone with my husband and I love him so deeply and I think we made it, we're going to be ok.

So as I said earlier in this book one of the strongest emotions through this entire mess was that I felt completely alone. It felt like no matter who I talked to they wanted to say the right thing or would just plain out say leave him. Neither of those did I need. I wish I had been able to read the stories of others that had been through some of the same experiences. To know that there may not be a fix out there but that time does go on and the initial devastating feeling where your stomach falls on the floor and you feel like you are going to throw up or pass out does go away. I don't think the hurt ever will be gone when the betrayal crosses your mind now and then over time but I am hoping it will cross my mind less and less as time goes on.

I guess the hardest part after the initial settles down is the not knowing. Not knowing what comes next. He is very attentive in the aftermath but is that going to last only long enough until his guilt goes away and his wanting to fix things is no longer there? Then does he just turn into the person he has been. He tells me this has changed him and he is going to do all he can to not only be a better man for me but to be a better man to me as well. For the most part things are ok given the circumstances but I really wish he would try to be there when those triggers come up instead of rolling over and going to sleep and leaving me to lay there with my own ghosts until exhaustion takes me to sleep. I guess there is the question everyone keeps asking me "why are you still there?" It seems to be the question that I don't have the answer to. There is so much involved. I love him. I have spent twenty years with him. I was raised you don't quit on a marriage just because things get tough, you work through it. I guess because even after all of this I don't want anyone else. There is so much right about him but then there is this side that tears me apart. I have decided that it takes more than love for a marriage to work. I guess I should have known this all along. I am still trying to put us back together. But I must admit I do feel like I am in it alone a lot of the time. I wish he would understand that I can't just forget and move on that I need to heal and he needs to rebuild my faith in him, in us and he needs to slowly show me that he will be faithful and that it is me he loves and this kind of devastation doesn't just heal overnight, it will take time.

I have talked to my husband and I have told him, no more. I just won't allow myself to live through this one more time. I have told him I don't trust him, he is the one that needs to earn that back. I have told him that there will be no more women. If I ever find out that he has had anything and I mean anything across that line with another woman again that I will leave him that day and that I will move away from the area and that I will immediately commence divorce proceedings because there will be no turning back, not again. So that if he ever is tempted by whoever it may be again, he had better factor me in this time because he will be throwing away everything that he has and that he had better make damn sure she is worth it. Should this be my fate, I know that this will be the hardest thing that I have ever have to do in my life and I also know that it is something that I will never accomplish on my own. I will call in any resources I can find to help me get through it but I will not allow myself to be here again. I barely made it out alive this time and it's not over yet. I still have hope we will get through this and that it really has changed who he is and that now he sees what devastation something of this magnitude can cost.

Again, only time will tell. It is he that has the choices to make.

Chapter Fifteen

The Fallout

So the next chapter beings in this twisted saga. Mark and I were working through the infidelity with Penny and I was adjusting to the foster kids being removed and the drop in income. After all I still had my job at the law office so I wasn't completely dependent. This went on without too much chaos for about seven months as the kids were removed in June. We were advised that there was a police investigation underway and that Penny had reported the incident to the Children's Aid Society who then reported it to the local police force. We were shocked to say the least.

We found out about this because her boyfriend was sending me threatening texts and voicemails saying he was going to get even and he would find my two boys and take care of them I think were his words. He said that my husband was a pedophile and that he and Penny were reporting him to the CAS and the police and that he would pay for what he did. Now this had us confused and a little angry to say the least as what took place with Penny was consensual and she was two months from being nineteen. Now I'm in no way trying to insinuate that what he did was in any way right it was so wrong there are no words. But in my opinion the only one he had wronged was me, his wife, with his infidelity. What he did was not illegal. But Penny painted the picture like this:

Penny gave a statement to the police saying that it was the day she was to get her braces on that Mark was home and he was to take her to the appointment. She said she was in the shower when he came into the bathroom wearing a towel. He watched her shower and she said she tried to hide in the corner but he stayed and watched anyway. When she got out of the shower he told her she should give him oral sex and that it was ok because he loved her. She said she felt obligated so did give him the oral sex in the bathroom for about 3 or 4 minutes then stopped. They went to the appointment and when they came home he sat on the couch and she again gave him oral sex. She said he tried to push her to have intercourse with her but she pushed him away. She said that he told her he wanted to give her pleasure to. She said that she was very uncomfortable and that she didn't want what was happening and the only reason she did it was that she felt obligated to.

However, on the stand she did admit that she had joked with Mark for over a year that she would give him oral sex as her going away present when she went off to college. She also told the police that there were times at parties where he would grab both her and Tracey by the breast or the buttocks. I found this part hard to believe because during the time that Tracey lived with us we had no parties at our house other than New Years Parties that my son had and Tracey and Penny were not present. She also told the police that Mark had showed her a sex tape of him and I and she described the tape in detail. She said that I provided her with alcohol and that I had purchased her sex toys for Christmas. I will admit at Christmas we used to buy joke gifts for all the teenagers and one year because Penny was so promiscuous and open about her sexual behaviour I bought her what is called a silver bullet as a joke. It is a miniature vibrator, she was eighteen. She knew at the time the gift was a joke. It wasn't until she wanted evidence to give to the police that she painted it otherwise.

There was also the incident of her birthday when she turned 19. Now you must remember my house was very sexually liberated and open when it came to joking about sex. Penny was adamant that for her nineteenth birthday she wanted a penis cake and she actually went to Aren't we Naughty and purchased a mould to make the cake and she iced the cake herself. Well when it came time for the statement to the police she told them that we surprised her with a penis cake in front of her new boyfriend and she was so humiliated. There were a lot of lies that Penny told, too many to write about, but I can say for sure I was even more hurt than I was before.

How could she not only cheat with my husband but then she had to lead the police to believe that our home was not a good home and we should be criminally charged and foster care taken away was just beyond what I imagined her capable of. It just didn't make sense considering Penny stayed in my home for four years on her request. Why did she have to go after me as well? What had I done other than not leave Mark and go to her like she had expected me to do?

We found out that all of the other foster children we had ever cared for were being questioned about the care provided in our home. They were also interviewing our friends. The rumour around town after the adult parties we had in the past was that Mark and I were swingers. Some people were trying to indicate that we allowed the foster teens to attend these parties.

Then the bomb dropped. It was January 20th at 6:30 a.m. I awoke to lights in my driveway which I noticed from my bedroom window. I looked out the window and all I could see were police lights and six police cruisers in my driveway and I heard the doorbell. I woke Mark up and said you better get up the police are here. I went downstairs and I answered the door in my housecoat and they showed me a piece of paper and said they had a search warrant to search the premises and asked if Sydney Mason (my husband's first name) was home. I advised them that he was and started to walk upstairs and they followed me up.

Mark was coming out of the bedroom and on his way down the stairs. At this time the female officer said to me "Ms. Mason you are under arrest for the sexual exploitation of Penny Greene." I said "you're kidding right. I never touched Penny or any other female for that matter". I was shocked that I was being charged at all. Then I heard a loud bang come from the stairway and saw that Mark had fainted and hit the floor. The police were trying to revive him and I heard them say that he was being charged with three counts of sexual assault. I tried to go to him but the female officer wouldn't allow me anywhere near him. They called an ambulance to take him to the emergency room to have him checked out in case.

She told me to get dressed I was going to the police station. I walked to my room and she followed me and watched me get dressed. It was so embarrassing to have someone especially a police officer stand there and watch you naked while you dressed. My mind was reeling still not understanding what was going on.

They took me to the Police station in handcuffs and took me in the back entrance and put me in a cell. I had never even seen the inside of a police station before in my life. I remember feeling surreal. I paced in the cell back and forth and it wasn't very big. It was all cement including the small bed which was just a cement shelf against the wall. No mattress no nothing. There was a toilet against the wall in plain view. I remember walking back and forth and counting my steps to keep myself from thinking. I told them my lawyer's name and they said they would call her. She eventually called and they put me in this little room about three feet by three feet with a telephone and a door so you can speak privately to your lawyer. My lawyer advised me to say nothing when questioned absolutely nothing. She would be at my bail hearing that day. I was crying but said ok.

I was scared I had never been in trouble before. They took me back to my cell and after a while I was brought to a little room with a one way mirror and a table and two chairs and a dvd player set up with a cd case they had taken from my home with a homemade dvd in it.

When they searched my home they took my brand new computer of three weeks, two external hard drives, Mark's laptop, my digital camera, my dvd camera, all my homemade dvd movies and picture cd's and photo albums.

While I was in this little room for questioning this officer in a suit came in. He started to make small talk like he was on my side. He offered me coffee or a bagel if I was hungry. This by now was about 11:00 a.m. Then he started asking me questions about the parties that took place in my home where there was nudity and sex. I did say that no sex ever took place at any parties at my home. He said everyone knew that my husband and I were swingers and I replied that I had never been with another man since the day I met my husband and we were not swingers. He tried to push me to admit that minors were at these parties and that I was having sexual relations with minors in my home and that my husband was sexually involved with minors. All I remember was I kept saying no comment. He said he was trying to help me and this was my chance to give my side of the story. I kept saying no comment.

It was about 2:00 p.m. when they came and put me back in hand cuffs and shackles and told me I was being transferred to Belleville for my bail hearing. When I arrived they put me in a cell where there was one other girl and across from us was the cell where the men were kept there was about ten of them at the time. She asked me what I was there for and I said a foster daughter had made false allegations against me. I asked what she was there for and she showed me a knife wound on her leg that she received in a domestic with her husband. I remember seeing them bring Mark down the stairs but because they said we could have no contact they couldn't put him in the cell beside me so they put him on a chair around the corner.

When it came time for us to go to the court room it was just after 3:00 p.m. They shackled my feet and hand cuffed my hands and led me upstairs. Now that is hard to do, walk upstairs with shackles on your feet. Anyway I walked into the court room and was put in the prisoner's box and when I walked in I saw my sister Barb sitting there and my son Doug as well as Mark's mother and sister. The Judge and the lawyers talked back and forth and they decided to delay bail for one day as it was late in the day and advised me that I would have to spend the night at the local jail in Napanee and return for a bail hearing the next day.

Now one thing I must mention is that I am very claustrophobic and they took me and this other girl out to the cube van which was divided into four compartments. She and I were in the front compartment and it was about two and a half feet wide and about six feet long. It was dark and there was no window. I could see a little out the front windshield of the truck but that was it. I felt like I was going to suffocate. I couldn't breathe. Before getting in I told the officer I was claustrophobic and was there a larger compartment I could be transported in. He said this isn't a taxi and pushed me inside.

I tried for the half hour ride to focus on the front window. It got really bad when we got there and he turned the engine off and the fan stopped because I felt like my breath stopped to.

When he took me from the van he took me through the front door of the prison to the desk where I was supposed to register. Register, it sounds like I was signing into a motel. From where I sat when I looked to my left I could see Mark in a cell looking at me and I saw him mouth the words I love you to me as I sat and cried my way through the registration. The officer asked if I had ever been in jail before and I said I had never been in trouble before. He asked if I wanted protective custody given my charges he thought it best. So I said ok.

Then a female office took me to change and search me. The change room was about six feet from the registration desk. It was an old bathroom with no door. She told me to take my clothes off, all of them, and I could see the male guards walking by looking at me which I thought was not only humiliating but illegal but they didn't seem to care. She told me to hold my breasts up and open my mouth and then to spread my legs, squat and cough. Then she gave me a track suit to wear. As she walked me down the hallway to my cell she asked what my charges were and I said I would rather not say. She said she could find out on the computer anyway and I said I would rather she did that. She said people like you are disgusting plain disgusting.

She then walked me through a steel door and two doors down the corridor and she unlocked the door to my cell and sent me inside for the night. It was about eight feet wide and ten feet long. It had two beds in it again cement beds. The mattress was about two inches thick and you were given one blanket and no pillow. It was January and freezing in there. There was another woman in the cell with me. She was Muslim and in on murder charges but was very good to me. I didn't get much sleep that night to say the least.

The next morning they again transported me to Belleville for my bail hearing. The transportation was just as bad as the night before. When I was taken into the court room I was granted bail with my sister Barb as my surety. I was released to her but on the condition that I have no contact with any of what they called my victims which was my 25 previous foster children or my own two biological sons or Mark. It was at this time my lawyer told me the Crown Attorney wasn't interested in me that in Canada you cannot be forced to testify against your husband so I was charged so she could make a deal she would drop the charges if I would agree to testify against Mark.

I went home with Barb and did a lot of crying. We went to my house so I could pack some clothes to take to her house. I don't remember much about the time I spent there I think I have blocked most of it out as I was in shock. I remember being at work the next week and getting a call from the Crown Attorney saying that Barb could not be my surety because she was a witness and that I needed to find another surety or I was going to spend my time until trial in the Napanee jail. I was panicked because everyone I knew either had kids and one of my conditions was I couldn't be around anyone under 18 or they were on my no contact list.

I called my step-mother as she lived alone because my father had just passed away and asked her if I could stay with her. She said no she didn't like living with anyone. So I talked to my lawyer and we went back to court. He managed to convince the Judge that since I owned my own home in the community and had full time employment I was not a flight risk so he allowed me to be on bail on my own recognisance. I was so happy I got to go home. I was going to be alone but I would be at home.

The police did a curfew check about once sometimes twice a week at my home as my curfew was 10:00 p.m. I didn't mind so much as I always went to bed early anyway but I found it very unprofessional that when they came to do the curfew check they made a point of putting the roof lights on while they drove down my 250 foot driveway. There was no need to put such a display on for my neighbours to see.

The publicity was community wide. We were on every radio station and in every local paper. They listed our names and ages and address for everyone to hear. We are from a small community so this is so bad. I continued to go to work and we had a buyer for our house which was to close in April. We also owned a little house in a town close to where we lived, I call it my cottage. I planned to move there and wait until Mark could come home again. Mark and I were apart for five months with no communication except what we could manage through his mother which wasn't much.

In April I moved into my little cottage and early May the Crown Attorney allowed Mark to move home as they were finished with their investigation. At one point during their investigation Mark worked for a local transport company and we used to get rid of our garbage in the big bin behind the plant he drove for. One night he threw out some garbage and in that garbage was my photo album from my first wedding and some old video tapes. Someone from the plant he worked at called the police and told them they saw Mark getting rid of video tapes so they actually went to where he worked and confiscated the entire garbage hopper to go through the garbage to try and find evidence.

The day Mark came home was a happy day in all this mess because it meant I didn't have to go through it alone anymore but I was also angry that I had been charged at all and I knew that none of this would have even been taking place had Mark just had the willpower to say no to Penny that one day.

One day at work I got a call from my lawyer and he asked me to come to his office and to bring someone with me. I took my friend Lisa and when we got there he told me to sit down and then he proceeded to advise me that I was being charged with twenty-six additional charges and that the Crown Attorney was asking for eight years in prison. I nearly fainted. I couldn't believe it. When I read the charges they stemmed from sexual exploitation because I bought the vibrator as a joke for Christmas to invitation to sexual touching because there was an allegation that I had given oral sex to a foster male in my home to possession of child pornography. Some of the charges were duplicates. He said he had seen the evidence and believed we could get a lot of the charges dropped before trial and could fight the rest at that time with a good chance of winning. Mark was charged with just as many charges as I was.

Mark's three sexual assault charges were: 1. the oral sex with Penny; 2. apparently Kerri said that when Mark bought her the car and told her she didn't have to pay for it that he said that she could just flash him instead one day; and 3. was one day Mark was getting ready for work and the kettle was boiling for his coffee and Tracey was standing by the counter. He reached around her to unplug the kettle and his arm brushed the edge of her breast. He said he didn't want to embarrass her so he made a joke of it and said "oh thanks." That was assault number three.

We had numerous meetings with our lawyers who told us not to worry it would all turn out. They told us the only thing the Crown had for sure was Mark on the oral sex thing with Penny. Well the time came for pre-trial.

Day one, one of Gary' friends (the foster child I apparently gave oral sex to) was on the stand and said that Gary told him I did this and was bragging about it. My lawyer asked him when this was and he replied that it was the night that he and Gary broke into a local youth club. The funny part of his story was the reason Gary came to my home was because of that break in. I didn't even know Gary during that time so it was impossible for Gary to have told him that. The next one to take the stand was a previous foster boy named Richie. Richie had charged the ex-friend of mine I talked about Claire with two counts of sexual assault, he claimed she gave him a hand job in our hot tub. This never took place as he was never at the house during the time she hung out there. He gave a huge statement to the police saying how we allowed all the kids to drink alcohol anytime and we spent their allowance on alcohol and that there was nudity at the house in front of him and a lot more. Now the reason Richie made this statement was because he made a deal with the Crown because he was charged with first degree murder at the time and was awaiting trial. They made a deal with him that if he testified against us and gave them information they needed and wanted they would work a deal for second degree and fifteen years. So he took the deal. Once he got on the stand he totally changed his story and said it was a great place to live and nothing wrong ever took place there. The problem with that is the Crown used him as a hostile witness and just played the video tape of his statement so that didn't help us.

Then the next one to take the stand was Penny. Of course she put on a great show with the tears and all. She had to take a break because she couldn't talk. Then they took a break for the day.

The second day before we were to enter the court room our lawyers took us each to a separate room and advised us the

Crown Attorney was offering a deal. By the way they were looking originally for ten years from Mark.

The Crown said that she was willing to accept three and a half years in prison for both of us and that we both plead guilty to the three charges she picked. Now for Mark she picked the three sexual assaults. For me she picked the sexual exploitation, householder allowing sexual activity and possession of child pornography.

Now the child pornography charge I should explain. I may have written about it before but I will explain it again. Doug and his girlfriend Faith went to a hotel in Toronto for a weekend when they were both twenty-three and Doug took naked pictures of her and put them on a cd. He asked me to lock up the cd as he didn't want the foster kids getting their hands on it. I never looked at the disc as I had no interest it was not my business. I just locked it up. Apparently on this disc there was four pictures of Faith when she was two weeks from eighteen which in the eyes of the law made her a child and since I was in possession of the disc that put me in possession of child pornography.

Now she had statements from both Doug and Faith saying they were responsible for the disc that I didn't even know what was on it. So the Crown had the ammunition that she needed.

I should also mention that the Crown charged Wayne with sexual assault on Jordanna who was his girlfriend at the time saying she was underage. She was 19 as well and they charged my friend Karen with sexual assault because there was a picture of Gary playing pool and Karen reaching down to the floor by him and it looked like her hands were between his legs as he was one of those teens that wore the baggy pants hanging low, so they said she was touching him. She wasn't. Anyway we said we didn't want to take the deal and that's when we were advised that if we took the deal she would drop all charges against our friends and after Mark asking to give him more time and me less she said she would let him do four years and me three years if we agreed.

She said if we didn't take the deal that she prepared that if we said no that she was going to charge Doug with production of child pornography because he took the pictures of Faith and that she had both of their statements as proof so he would for sure serve two years.

Now as a mother the Crown knew that I would never send my son to jail and that I would do anything to keep them safe. So I felt like I had no alternative but to take the deal and serve the three year sentence. I had no idea what I was getting myself into.

We took the deal On October 1st and were to be sentenced on November 1st. That gave Mark and I one month together and then we would be separated for more than three years this time not voluntarily.

I don't remember much about that month it just seems like a blur to me.

Chapter Sixteen

The Transition

Well November 1st arrived and far too fast. I remember we had been living at Mark's mother's upstairs apartment for the month because we knew we were going away for quite a while and we rented out our home for the duration.

Mark's sister walked to the court house with us. When we arrived we were sitting waiting to go in and Penny walked in she was looking better than usual she had lost a lot of weight but this was due to her continued drug use, she had now since moving out gotten involved in the heavier drugs like cocaine. She wore a short black mini skirt and a white see through shirt with about 6" heels on her shoes. I wanted to hate her so much yet all I could feel when I looked at her was jealousy and I kept telling myself no wonder he turned away from me and turned to her, look at her, she's absolutely beautiful.

We met with our lawyers and signed the paperwork to agree to the terms of the deal. My two boys were at the court house as well. When we entered the court room and sat down the Judge and the lawyers did some talking then we were told to stand while the Crown read her statement of facts. What a tough thing to listen to. 95% of the information she read to the court were fabrications and lies and we had no choice but to listen. Because we made a deal with the Crown and agreed to plead guilty that meant we were not entitled to give any defence to any of the charges so she was free to read any facts she wanted to and then the Judge read out the three charges that both Mark and I had pled to and again after hearing everything the Crown had read what we had supposedly done we had to stand in a crowded court room and say guilty when the charges were read out.

We weren't able to say to the people in the court room or the press there taking notes "hey we didn't do this stuff we were blackmailed into taking a deal to save our son." So then the Judge read his notes on his opinion of us and let's just say he was very harsh. I started having a panic attack in the court room so I took one of my prescribed demerals which usually helped, it didn't this time. After the Judge read his statement we were told to go up and stand by the prisoner's box to be taken for DNA samples and to be made ready for transport. I remember standing there by that box and I looked back and the last thing I saw was my two precious sons looking at me sadly mouthing the words I love you to me and I could have cried or given anything to give them one more hug. That picture would remain in my eyes for a very long time.

Then they took us to the back of the court room where there was a jail cell and a desk and an officer. We were asked one at a time to come to the desk, where he pricked your figure for a blood sample so that we would be on the DNA registry. One other condition that was imposed by the Crown was because we were charged with sexual offences against minors we are now registered on the Provincial and Federal Sexual Offenders Registry for the rest of our lives. We have to appear at the local police station once a year to report any changes in our appearance or if we change our address we have to report it. There are no conditions as far as being around children or playgrounds or where we could live so I was at least grateful for that because I couldn't imagine finally having grandchildren and not being able to babysit them alone. Thank God for small favours. This was so wrong. I didn't do anything wrong. This was so unfair.

Mark asked if we could have a few minutes to say good-bye. It's funny really when I think about it. Maybe it was the demoral I took or just shock but I just felt numb, not much of anything. We were standing in a jail cell and he hugged me and told me we would get through this and that he loved me. I said I loved him to and then the female officer came to get me and put me in handcuffs and led me out the back door. When I was being driven out of the parking lot I saw Kerri standing there watching the cruiser leave and smiling like she had won some big prize.

I watched as the scenery went by on my way to Napanee jail knowing what I was about to face but I thought I would be there a few days then transferred to the Federal Prison known as Grand Valley Institute for Women. I was wrong. They again processed me and put me through the strip search and led me to my protective custody cell. I was put in the cell again with the same woman as before for my one night stay. She made things as easy on me as she could given the circumstances. I was held in Napanee for 17 days waiting for transport. I was eager for the transport because I was lead to believe that at Grand Valley you lived in a house with ten other women, did your own cooking, that it was like a community.

For the 17 days at Napanee I didn't eat much didn't have much of an appetite. My sister visited me once but I had to leave during the visit because I had such bad diarrhea, I think from nerves it was so bad. I was freezing all the time and I couldn't sleep. Every night I went to sleep I had the same dream over and over again. I dreamt I was leaving the court house and I had to say good-bye to my kids all over again only in my dream my boys were little only 3 and 5. I would wake up with tears on my face. I had the same dream every night.

Well day 17 came and they told me I was being transported, I thought to Grand Valley but apparently I had to spend some time in Lindsey jail first another provincial institute. I was there for 19 days. At Lindsey I was again in protective custody. I didn't leave my cell at all at any time for the 19 days. They were crowded so I was put in a room with another girl it was about ten feet by ten feet there was no bed. We were given a two inch mattress on the floor and a toilet against the wall. Again it was surreal to me. It was like I was going through the motions but wasn't there at the same time.

You were allowed to shower if you wanted to but you were given about fifteen minutes and they gave you a clean track suit to wear. After day nineteen they told me I was being transported to Grand Valley. I was nervous but I thought I was ready. Anything had to be better than this.

This time they transported me in a large cube van all windows. When I got to Grand Valley they took me to an office where they took my picture and gave me my id and said I was to carry it with me at all times I was now an official number.

They gave me a plastic bag with a change of clothes, a blanket and pillow and a bowl, spoon, saucer and plate and a butter knife and fork and a few other incidentals. They gave me a budget of thirty dollars and told me to pick my groceries for the week from the list. At

Grand Valley you do live in a house with ten other women and each week you are given a budget of thirty dollars to buy your food for the week which you prepare for yourself. They told me I was to go to house number five.

When I arrived with my belongings I was shown to my room and on the way to my room one of the other women said they didn't want to share a house with a pedophile. I was scared. The house representative came to my room and asked that I tell her the truth of my story so she could go to the other house members and maybe get them to come around so I told her all I could. Eventually it wasn't too bad they didn't talk to me much but they didn't harass me either.

It was day three I went for a walk to what they called the logia which is where you get your mail and healthcare is housed and people just hang out. On my way home a group of girls started threatening me saying I was a child molester and that I had abused thirteen kids with beer bottles, where that came from I have no idea. They said the one of my foster kids, Gary, the one that was killed in the four wheeler accident, committed suicide because he couldn't stand the abuse and they just went on and on. I was afraid for my safety and went back inside my house.

I was later moved to another house and when I arrived with my belonging it was unreal. First they locked the door so I couldn't get in. I went and got a guard who opened the door and all the other nine women in the house were in the living room and they started yelling at me that they didn't want to share a house with a pedophile someone that would hurt children. They said they were mothers themselves and didn't have any respect for someone that would hurt a child. This harassment went on for over an hour. I was supposed to share a room with one of the girls but she refused so one of the other girls gave up her single room to me and shared a room with the girl who refused me.

I learned quickly to avoid contact with anyone. I made a deal with the house representative that if she came to my room for my order which was not much she could have the rest of my money. I only bought bread, margarine and bananas and for two years I never left my room unless I had to go pee which I made sure was only in the morning so I didn't drink much of anything or I got called to healthcare about my medication as I was put on strong antianxiety medication early on or if I had to go to the required sex offenders course. All the rest of the time was spent in my room. As bad as it sounds I was threatened so much that I actually went six months without a shower because I knew I had to leave my room and walk down the hall to the bathroom and they would be waiting for me.

There was a girl in the room across from me who was on methadone and was a heroin addict. She had severe mood swings. One day she started kicking my door and banging on the small window yelling "you're next, I'll get you next." I was so scared I just huddled in the corner of my bed and held my knees to my chest. Afraid to move.

I had a lot of time to think actually that's pretty much all I did until I just couldn't think anymore. The days dragged by so slowly it felt like I would never open my eyes again and not see that fence keeping me in.

Mark was as good as he could be he wrote me usually 5 at the least 4 letters per week and each letter was 10 pages long. They helped but made it hard at the same time because I was forced to remember him, the kids and home and I didn't want to, yet I so needed to know he still loved me that there would be an end to this nightmare, I just had to hold on. He made a lot of revelations during his time inside.

He realized that the mistakes that he made had everything to do with him and very little to do with me. He told me that he always believed from his childhood that he was never meant to be here. He was always told he wasn't wanted and that he wrecked his parent's marriage and he grew up believing that. That's why he drove his care carelessly as a teenager and adult, he got into fights at school, fights that weren't even his to fight because he was always angry and just didn't care if he got hurt. He told me he realized that he drove his car carelessly because he believed if he ended up having a car accident and was killed in the accident then all would be right because he shouldn't have been here in the first place.

He told me he was so sorry for the hurt that he had caused me and he realized that I was all that he wanted and that he would spend the rest of his life making this up to me and cherishing me. I had finally heard the words I had waited so many years to hear. I asked him if he would ever stray again and he said definitely not that he never wanted to carry the weight of that guilt again or to hurt me ever again. I was so happy to hear those words. Did I finally have the husband I always wanted?

Well I won't drag out the incarceration period of my life because that is not what this book is about but suffice it to say it was a nightmare that will live on in me for the rest of my life. I'm still fighting to get back to me, I still have triggers that put me back there but I'm a work in progress. I got out on Halloween and stayed at a half-way house until the following April. This was by choice as my house was rented and I wasn't sure how I would pay for it if I came back home.

I got notice that my tenants were moving out in April. So I thought if I was ever going to take the plunge back into the community this was the time, so I did. I moved home April 13th and for the very first time in my life to my humility I was forced to go on Ontario Works to help me pay the bills at my house because one of my conditions on parole was I was allowed no access to the internet so being employed in the field I was I was unemployable for the time being. So I went on Ontario Works which paid me $649.00 a month and the bills for my house were about $2,000 a month. I was very grateful that when we found out we were being sued for $14,000,000 that we maxed out the line of credit on our home and Mark's mother held the cash so it would be hidden. So I had approximately $12,000 because she divided the money separately for me and Mark, as she was doing her very best to get him to leave me and never come home and as she put it she didn't want me spending his money. So I used that saving for most of the year to help pay to keep me in the house.

In about December I got a job doing the books for a construction company under the table for $15 dollars an hour so that brought in about $1800 a month but it was only full time for about 3 months so after that I went to Career Edge and registered to attend college for my Small

Business Bookkeeping Certificate. I just graduated recently. However, I am finding it almost impossible to find employment as everywhere I apply needs a clear criminal record check. Even McDonalds. So with University courses under my belt a college degree and twenty years office experience, because my husband had to have that half hour of pleasure I am for the first time in my life unemployable and live in fear every day as to how I will pay my bills for the next month. I am again on Ontario Works receiving $646.00 per month as income. Mark has been helping by sending me money each month and I still have a small savings left. After that I don't know what I'll do to support myself.

Mark was released in July of 2014, which was almost a year and a half ago as now it is the end of January 2016. His condition was he wasn't allowed to see me and I wasn't allowed to see him. My conditions were over on Halloween so that meant other than the sex offender registry once a year I was finally free to try to start to live my life again.

He arranged a cell phone in his uncle's name and sent it down to me so we could talk on the phone and no one knew because his cell phone bill would only show calls between him and his uncle. It was amazing to be able to hear his voice and to talk to him, I missed him so much.

Now comes the part of the story where I may have destroyed my marriage and my life. Before Mark got out when I first came home I told you earlier I was so not me. I was a shell of a human being with no feelings and absolutely no emotion. I hadn't been able to cry for over three years. I believed this was going to be me for the rest of my life. I knew I loved my kids and my husband and I was so glad to be free yet I didn't feel the emotions that should have gone along with those blessings. I went through day to day numb I guess is the best way to describe what I felt like.

Anyway my best friend Karen knew this man named Seth. I had only met him once about 6 years ago. I knew he was attracted to me then because Karen used to tell me he was. I never once thought about him as any more than Karen's friend that I was introduced to.

When I was visiting Karen she said he had been asking about me and that she was going to be in town at her mother's house babysitting elderly people her mother takes care of and that Seth would be coming over to visit her and would like to see me so I went up for the visit.

 Now I should point out here that Karen and Seth had an affair that lasted about 3 years but both advised me that they were now just friends and hadn't been sexual in over 2 years. I noticed Seth was looking at me but was very shy. He stayed about 3 hours and we all just talked and laughed about stupid stories from our pasts. Before he left I don't know what I was thinking about but I invited Karen and Seth over to my house a couple of nights later for a few drinks and to hang out. They both said yes that would be great. Seth has a girlfriend that he loves but still said he would be there and we had talked while at Karen's mother's about when Mark came home I would be waiting for him because I still loved him heart and soul and I said how that would never change for me.

Well the night arrived when he came to visit. He got there about an hour before

Karen and we just put on some country music and talked. I noticed he kept looking at me and I was flattered given that instead of weighing 125 pounds I now weighed at least 160 at that time. I found his eyes and long hair attractive, I have always liked long hair on men, my husband was always known as the guy with the hair, anyway about 15 minutes before Karen was to arrive after Seth telling me how beautiful I was and that I had been his fantasy for over 6 years and that he couldn't believe that he was actually in my company and that I didn't need to lose a pound, that I was beautiful just the way I was, I got curious to see if I was even capable of ever feeling any emotion again so I did something really really stupid and something I will now pay for for the rest of my life. I moved over to where he was sitting on the couch and I straddled him on the couch and I kissed him. He was shocked at the kiss but welcomed it with passion. I felt so guilty. I found out that was one emotion I was capable of feeling and I got off his knee and sat beside him on the couch. I knew in my heart that what I had done was so wrong yet on the other hand I was grateful inside because I actually felt a small emotion. I felt desired and I felt like a part of me could maybe come back to life from that kiss so wrong as it was at the time.

I clung to that little bit of life. Karen arrived and the three of us talked until about Midnight. Karen had drank a bottle of wine and went to bed in the spare room about 12:30. Seth and I stayed up until about 3:00 am talking and then he leaned over and he kissed me passionately. I am not writing any of this in this book to hurt my husband's heart I did that completely from that first kiss on, but I have promised to be honest in this book and that means writing about my mistakes and flaws just as honestly as I have written about his. Seth and I laid beside each other on the couch and he caressed me. I was dressed. He kissed me and caressed me for hours and that was all he wanted. He didn't push sex with me and I would never have done that had he wanted it.

He was content to kiss me and hold me and kept telling me he couldn't believe his fantasy was in his arms. I felt for the first time since I don't remember when that someone had chosen me first, someone really wanted me and thought even fat I was desirable and sexy. I know this is so wrong but it gets worse. He spent the night sleeping on the couch and I slept in my bed.

When I got up the next morning he was talking to Karen having a cigarette. He didn't say much to me as he is very shy when he isn't drinking and I should point out here that Seth has a serious drinking problem and I knew that. It didn't matter to me because I was not in a relationship with him nor would I ever be. I loved my husband, we just had a lot in common and I enjoyed his company when he had drinks and the atmosphere of having drinks and loud music and kisses made me feel alive and as wrong as that was I was so desperate to feel alive, I clung to all of it.

When he left my house he asked me if he could text me and I said yes. So we started texting back and forth talking as friends but he did mention how he still felt like it was a dream that he had held his fantasy in his arms after all the years he had thought about me and that made me feel good. I didn't get to hear those words from Mark so I felt special.

I knew Seth was safe for me because he was never the type of man I would have a relationship with even if I was not married I knew I would never would be in a position to give any man my heart I gave that away a long time ago.

One Friday night he invited me out to a cottage where he lived for a bonfire. Where he lived there are seven cottages that a man rented out to different people. Usually people with addictions. I went to the cottage and had some drinks with Bryon. It was a fun night, something I hadn't experienced in a very long time. I actually had a few hours where my brain was on hold. I could just listen to the country music and enjoy the company of a man who seemed to want my company, who thought I was beautiful, who wanted to listen to what I had to say.

I was in a very vulnerable position and I am by no means here excusing the very bad judgment call I made by getting sexually involved with this man. But he made me feel alive again, happy for a moment and sexually attractive no matter what age I was.

I started spending a lot of time there almost every weekend. We became very close and shared a lot together, we talked about our pasts and he seemed to accept mine, flaws and all and loved me anyway in time. I knew he had a drinking problem but given all the support he gave me I accepted that and tried to be there for him.

We shared almost every weekend together throughout the summer and had a wonderful time. I was alive again. I had someone that wanted just me. He liked what I liked. There was only one thing wrong with the entire situation. I still loved my husband no matter what he had done and this never went away for me.

Well My husband got out of jail in July of that year and we started having secret conversations on the phone from someone that lived at the property. I loved him dearly but I was also drawn up in feeling passion again, having someone listen to me for a change and just having a party. After jail that's all that seemed to matter to me at the time. I was so wrong I know on the deepest level I betrayed my husband. I told him I would never find this man attractive. I said there was no one but him and never would be. I thought he would never know another man had given me something I so desperately needed at the time.

Well my world once again came crashing down. It was about 11 months since I started seeing this man. I had only seen my husband twice since he got out and we had a very wonderful time together although we didn't relate a lot. We had some drinks, had sex and watched t.v. There was no talking and I needed that to be important. To know he needed to reconnect with me on a deeper level. He didn't.

Anyway in April of that year, I went to Ottawa to change over the registration of my car back into my name from my son's and on the trip there I was texting this other man about our relationship and my feelings for him.

I went to see my husband that weekend and I had had a couple of drinks with him. I was told he knew about me and this other man and I was ready to talk about it. But I wanted to be prepared and make sure he knew it wasn't about him in so many ways. So I wrote an eight page letter to him telling him how quickly I fell in love with him twenty-four years ago and that this hadn't changed no matter what. What my feelings were for him and what had taken place with this man and why.

He wanted me to read the letter out loud so I did. When I was finished he sat quietly for a moment. Made no reply. Got up from the bed and went to the bag he had brought to the hotel. He took out some papers and he threw them at me and said I think you need to read this. I looked at it and my heart sank in my chest. He had a copy of the texts between me and this other man. I knew right away where he had gotten them from and had never felt so betrayed in my life.

I just looked at them and said nothing. He said read them and read them out loud. I said I think you have already read them there is no reason for me to read them out loud. I take it you received these from my son. He said my son hadn't given them to him he had just sent them to an email address he could access. I was so hurt. I knew I had done wrong but I had believed my son was my best friend. I never thought he would betray me to that degree that he would search through my cell phone, copy my texts and send them to my husband and not even give me a heads up he had done this. I was so hurt I couldn't even respond.

I left that weekend and nothing has been the same since. I have had no more contact with this man as my marriage is the most important thing to me. Although I feel it may be too late for that boat to sail. He hasn't seen me since May and when I ask when or if he will ever see me again all he says is I don't know. He talks about his future job and hobbies he wants to do but none seem to include me. When I ask him if there is room for me in his future his answer is I don't know, I'm just taking it day by day. This has now been going on for over 9 months. I have apologized, I have given him all passwords to any online site I have. I have begged and I have pleaded for him not to leave me just as I have done for the last 24 years. Nothing has changed.

For a while he said he doesn't know if he wants me yet he was calling me every day and talking to me like I'm his buddy. I don't want to be his buddy I want to be his wife. For a while he stopped saying I love you at the end of our phone calls and it didn't seem to hurt him to hurt me. He does it almost on a daily basis.

I asked him just last week if it matters to him if I'm in his life or not. His response was before yes now not so much. We were talking on the phone one night and I was excited because I had rented out our house because I knew he would never come back here and I had rented an apartment in a nearby town because he said one night he might consider living there. When I was telling him about it all on the phone I was getting one word answers that was it. I asked him if he was even interested in what I was telling him and he responded with "well some of it." Again he hurt my heart. I told him good-night and I would talk to him tomorrow. He was ok with that.

It has been a constant nine months of me beg and plead for any scrap of I love you as it's always been and him giving me nothing. I was crying on the phone the other day and explained this to him that I was emotionally running on empty that he hadn't said one kind thing to me in nine months. His explanation for this was I am an emotional person and if he says anything positive I will run with it and start telling him he committed to moving home. He said with me he has to operate on the premise that the glass is half full at all times. I was crying by this point which by the way I am so tired of doing. I said that's cruel. So you're telling me you want to say positive things to me you feel them but you don't say them. He said yes.

The next day I was doing some internet surfing and I found a book for men and how getting over an infidelity is very different from how a woman does it. So I ordered the e-book for me so I would know what he was going through and perhaps help him through it and I ordered him the audio book because he's not a big reader. He said he would give it a listen. As far as I know as of today he hasn't.

Well when I was done reading the book there were some things that really hit home for me about his affair with Penny and that I had never had closure from him on and some things I didn't agree with like he should stop being a doormat, he never was, and how he should stop saying I love you as often, he doesn't now, and how if he pulls away I'll want him more. If he pulled away any more he wouldn't be in my life at all. So I emailed him with my feelings.

A few hours later I thought better of it, because he doesn't have any interest on healing the hurt from Penny, he doesn't want to even hear about it because he just gets mad and says I'm pointing the finger at him when I am the cheater. I got worried about how he would take the emails I had sent and I had access to his Hotmail account so I logged in so I could delete the emails before he saw them but they had already been opened. Now this could mean one of two things either he opened and read them or he opened them saw they were long and closed them to look at later.

Well one day he was supposed to go up flying in a two seater plain at 8:30 this morning. By 4:00 I hadn't heard a word from him. I had deleted the emails by then. I texted him and told him that I had sent him two emails today and wanted to know if he had read them and how I was hoping he hadn't and that I was just having a weak moment. I told him if he hadn't I was going to delete them. He never responded. So I said are you still flying. Eventually he said no the weather was crappy. I was a little hurt because if he didn't go flying at 8:30 a.m. and it was 4:00 p.m. and he hadn't wanted to talk to me, well it hurt. So I sent a message before I received his next reply when I said are you busy or mad at me.

Apparently he had already sent I'm just folding laundry. I didn't get that message until I sent my next one. I said well if you get a chance let me know if you've read the emails I hope you haven't. I was completely shocked at his response. In the twenty-four years we have been together he has never spoken to me in this manner. He sent me a text that said "I said I was folding laundry....wholly fuck." I couldn't believe he would talk to me that way over a text. So I sent a response very simply saying "never-mind forget I said anything, that was completely uncalled for, have a good night." I knew when I said have a good night he would punish me by not calling and that is exactly what he did.

I have to quit playing this game and letting him treat me this way. I made a mistake, so has he, I'm trying all I can to make up for it but it doesn't give him the right to treat me any way he pleases because he's hurt.

I knew then that he wouldn't call me until I contacted him first which is what he always does. I have to find the strength someday to not give in and chase him. I cannot call him and beg him to talk to me again. This is going to be a very hard thing for me to do, I love him and I miss him, but he has said such hurtful things to me, I need to do some thinking. Is this what the rest of my life is going to be if he comes home? Is my marriage over because I made the mistake this time instead of him, the reasons don't matter to him.

I cannot call him until he gets in contact with me this time. I have to hold my ground and if he chooses to not contact me then I have my answer about how much I actually really did mean to this man.

When he went with not talking to me last time for four days I gave in and texted him and said I miss talking to you. He called that night. I said if I hadn't called would you have called me. He said probably not. I said would I have ever heard from you again. He answered "oh maybe eventually, I'm not sure." He really doesn't care how much he hurts me. Now I'm not sure if this is just his personality or the fact that he is a narcissist and a sociopath. The question I need to ask myself at this point is whether or not this is how I want to live the rest of my life, being talked to rudely, told I don't matter as much and he could take our relationship or leave it, it didn't really matter one way or the other.

I think I already know the answer to that logically the problem is getting the message to a heart that has loved him for twenty-six years.

I told myself I will not give in this time and call him first. I need him for once to come to me and if he chooses not to then I guess I have my answer and I need to find a way through the trauma and the heartache I know I'm going to feel but yet I've done nothing but cry for the last three days anyway as I pack my stuff to move out of our home and leave the last little bit of him behind. But he doesn't care, it doesn't bother him at all.

Well it's now November, Christmas is approaching fast. We started talking again I haven't written in a while so I'm not exactly sure how that came about. I moved into my new apartment on October 12th my sons helped me move. It was bittersweet because it was a new start but I had left all my memories behind in my home. My only hope was he would join me in my apartment and make this our new home together.

We had been talking every day but not for long periods of time mostly he would call to say good night or talk to me on his way home from work for about 15 minutes.

I had decided to put up my first Christmas tree in five years because I said I would not put one up until he came home but that didn't seem to be happening and I didn't know if it ever would. I picked November 14th to put the tree up and my son Ryan and my sister Barb came over to watch me put it up so I wasn't alone. But I missed Mark so much. I sent him pictures that night of the tree and he said it looked like fun.

I had invited him at the beginning of October to join us on tree night, he kept saying I'll let you know. It was about a week before when I asked if he was coming or not. He said he didn't think it was a good idea. I said why not? He said well if I decide I don't want to continue with this marriage, I don't want to look like a dick to the boys. I said you're still thinking that. He said yes. So he never came.

I asked him if he would be coming home for Christmas with the family. He said well I think they are doing something here and I don't want to look like the outsider. I said so you're picking your aunt and uncle over your family. He said well I don't think it's a good idea.

I kept trying. I said well if you don't want to look like a dick to the boys will you consider spending New Years Eve with just me. We can have a drink, watch some movies, cuddle and talk. It could be a new beginning. He said that sounds nice ma. (That's what he calls me). I said so you'll really think about it. He said yes. I was happy maybe he was coming around.

I got very lonely one night and sad looking at the Christmas tree all lit up and being alone all the time. He called and I was crying on the phone. He said what do you want from me. I said attention something anything, something positive. I said are you ever coming home? He said well I don't think with the state you're in this is the time to get into it. I said well if it was good news you would tell me to make my day better the only reason you won't say anything is because it's bad news. All he said was I don't agree and the phone call ended.

Starting the next day I really believed he was putting in the effort and he was coming around. He started calling me seven or eight times a day. He was nice. At the end of our phone calls when I said I love you he said it back. At the end of our good night call I would say "think about me a little." He replied "I always do." Which was something he always used to say to me and hadn't in a long time. I took it as a very good sign.

One day on the phone I told him I was so tired of being lonely that I spend every day here alone missing him. He said the days are the same for me. Again he gave me hope. He was coming around I thought it was only a matter of time.

Then he had to go to emergency to see about getting some antibiotics for an infection and they said it was a trauma center and that he needed a Dr. He said his Dr. was three hours away so the emergency Dr. gave him a card for a Dr. up there that was taking new patients. He was talking to me about it after he went to the office and said he was told to get this Dr. to take him on he had to cut ties with his Dr. here. I said well that's crazy because if you come home you won't be able to go back to our family Dr. Why don't you just make an appointment to come down and see your Dr. here since you are now laid off for the winter. I nearly fell over at his answer. He said "why would I want to drive three hours just to see a Dr." I couldn't believe it I thought he would come and see me for a day or two and see the Dr. when he was here. I said well if that's how you're looking at it get a Dr. there. I said I can't help but feel like you're stringing me along. He said I don't agree I'm just doing day by day. I said no you're not you told your boss you would be coming back next year. You told your winter employer you would be there all winter. You're now training the men you work with at the gym and now you're getting your Dr.

moved up there. What are you doing? He said I can't get into this right now. So I said well call me later and it's about time you started doing some talking. I think you already know your answer you're just not telling me. He said ok.

Well it was 10:15 that night and I hadn't heard from him since noon. So I called and I said am I on ignore now. He said well I had supper and watched some tv and fell asleep. I said so what are you doing Mark. He said I want you to finish school and become self-sufficient and move on with your life. I said you're never coming home are you. He said "no." I was so hurt I didn't know what to do so I just hung up the phone and cried.

I had my answer. I had lost my husband, my love, the man who raised my children. My other half. Our story was over. Where do I go from here?

Well I got up the next day and just felt empty and sad like my whole world had just turned upside down and I didn't know where to go or what to do. I cried for about an hour and looked around the house at the pictures and the memories we shared. I took down the poem he wrote me years ago that I had hanging on my wall and put it away in my hope chest with his pictures. Still crying. I texted friends just to not feel so alone. I went on my facebook and deleted all his pictures crying the entire time.

I was hoping so much he would call that day to see how I was and change his mind but he didn't and he won't. He made his decision, he doesn't want me anymore. I've lost him.

I was numb most of the day tried to get lost in tv but it didn't work. Then a friend called to check on me and I started crying all over again for another hour or so. I would have given anything to hear Mark's voice and have him tell me he still loved me. I was wracked with guilt all day because I brought this on myself, I made a mistake and betrayed the man I have loved half my life and now I lost him. I hate myself for it.

My problem now is nothing even looks the same. Everything feels cold and lonely and I'm so afraid I'll never feel loved again that I'll be alone for the rest of my life because of what I did. I don't think I'll ever love anyone else ever again so I guess

I'll be one of those old ladies still in love with their ex-husbands until I die. Sad but probably true.

I applied for a name change because all the criminal charges were made so public on the internet I can't find work. Hoping to leave my past in the past, but another part of him I had to let go, his name. Welfare which I have never needed in my entire life now looks like my only option and they pay $646.00 per month. My rent if $939. Not to mention other bills. Mark has been sending me $1000 a month but I imagine that is now going to stop. I don't know what I am going to do.

My friends say I'm better off without him that he was toxic to me. But I love him and I miss him and I'm so broken right now I don't even know where to look first. I just wish I could sleep until I don't hurt anymore but sleep seems to evade me to.

I know he's never coming back to me our story has reached its end.

So I guess it's the end of my book, I started with does love conquer all, well I guess the answer would be no, no it doesn't sadly. At least not for me.

I hope you have enjoyed reading my journey and if you have gone through something similar I hope you had a happier result than I did. I don't think I'll ever be the same but I do know the sun will come out tomorrow and the next day and maybe someday I'll wake up and not cry and I won't be counting how many days it's been since I heard his voice. That I will just start to forget to count. That I won't miss the sound of his voice and I will be able to look at his pictures again and not hurt and cry.

He was my heart and soul, the love of my life, my soul mate. Father to my boys. Now he will be that to someone else someday. I just hope he can look back on our twenty six years and remember some good times and good memories and not hate me when he thinks about me.

I know I'll love him forever.

Thanks for listening.

Janet

If you have been through a similar situation or just have a comment for me please email me at sensuousraven@gmail.com. I would love some advice or just to hear someone else's story and help if I can with the process.

Chapter Seventeen

Conclusion

The Final Chapter:

It wouldn't be fair to take you on my journey only to leave you with the conclusion being the infidelity.

In the aftermath of my finding out about the final affair, it was a tumultuous road and what felt like a long one. I guess I'm still on that road and one thing I have figured out is nothing is definite when it comes to the heart.

However, I must give my husband the credit he is due. There are two ways for your husband to react to your emotions and the guilt and shame they carry from the infidelity and knowing that they have hurt the one person they truly love.

One, they can refuse to accept responsibility and ownership for the hurt and damage that their actions have caused and two, they can accept responsibility for their actions and they can man up and do whatever is necessary to get you to that place where you can slowly and timidly try to open up your heart to them again and learn to trust in your relationship again. My husband after his final affair, finally, chose the latter of the two.

That was until the tables turned and I made the same mistake, then it was a different story. He was no longer able to forgive. In his eyes I betrayed him and that was unforgiveable. I guess to a man at least to mine I was now damaged goods. It's funny how he expected each and every time to be forgiven and knew somehow that I would never give up on him. I don't understand why I wasn't given the same devotion.

I had reasons or as most people will think excuses to turn to someone else. He did this when we were happy there were no reasons other than lust and I forgave. Why couldn't he? He gave up 26 years together because his pride was hurt and his manhood bruised.

I realized after my mistake of turning to another man who would give me what Mark would not that it didn't matter I stilled loved Mark. I can't love anyone else. And as much as there are things that I would like him to do which I believe would make this process easier to get through, I have to accept the fact that just as I couldn't control his choices to cheat or not to cheat, I cannot make him be the person I want him to be at all times. I can't make him be romantic and write me letters and I can't make him soft and emotional and want to share his feelings either. I knew when I married him he was a man's man. He was strong and didn't show his weaker emotions. He was taught very young that this was not ok to do and he learned at a very young age to disconnect from the heart. I guess it is for those reasons that he cannot completely let down those walls just because I want him to.

I have been on a long road with Mark but even though there have been moments of infidelity and hurt, there have also been so many moments of pure happiness. It is those moments that make it all worth it. It is those moments that I was fighting for. Those moments that make it not easy to walk away. I know that he loved me as much as sometimes his actions indicate otherwise. He was just not willing to forgive me to keep us together, he chose to walk away, I chose to stay. As I said each person makes a different decision. I married this man for better or worse. He apparently had another idea.

One thing I have learned over time and all the hurt we have both caused each other is that time does not heal all wounds no matter what you hear. As much as we would all like to think that everything is in the past and we would like to choose to leave it there, this is not something that is always a choice. Sometimes we react instinctively and then after we have already felt the little stab that comes along with old hurts we can then choose to say to ourselves "no I'm not going back there" which is great except you have already felt the hurt again.

I'm not sure you can expect that just because you have made the choice to remain together that you will no longer carry with you the history that the two of you have made together because you will. I also believe that history is so important and just like any story it can't be all good but I tend to believe that even though there are those moments of temporary flash backs to the past there are also a lot of moments that cause you to think about the past and all the good memories that you have made together. I guess what I am trying to say is in order to rebuild after infidelity you have to be ready to take the good with the bad because there will be both and that it takes a conscious effort not to throw the past in the face of your spouse when you are angry or they say something hurtful towards you. It is those times that you have to take a step back and remind yourself what it was like without that person that makes up the other half of you and then maybe it is a little easier to take a deep breath and remind yourself that perception is not always fact and just because your spouse may be having a bad day doesn't mean you have to jump aboard and turn his bad day into a rip roaring fight.

I am finding that it seemed to work better for me if when he was with me when he was having an off day to let him vent and not say much of anything except maybe to give him a hug and tell him I love him and give him time to get himself out of that mood and more times than not he will come to me later and tell me he is sorry and that he loves me. This was rather new to me as I was always a person who was very much a right fighter and speaking from experience when you have two right fighters no one wins. It is sometimes still a challenge for me but I like to consider myself still a work in progress. I know I still have a lot of healing to do now that he has chosen to leave me and not forgive me and I know it won't be an easy road nor will it be a short one.

One thing I have found to be hard is the mind set of Mark. I forgave him because I loved him so much more than I hated what he had done. Why didn't he love me that much? I made one mistake in 26 years and he walks away from me. He said he has to think about not only what's best for him but what's best for me and maybe being together isn't the best thing. That we have separated in the past. What's best for me is us, my marriage, he was my life and I'm afraid always will be, here or not. I wish he would have had it in his heart to forgive me and come home where he belongs, but I can't make him want me and I can't make him forgive and I certainly can't demand he come back to me. I'm just very sad that he has made the decision to walk away from a lifetime together when we still have time left to grow old together, to be happy, to learn from our mistakes and be a stronger couple for it. But that is just my perspective, I never was able to just give up. My parents were married for 53 years and I was taught marriages go through tough times, some you think you may never survive, but that's what makes a life time marriage, you work at it, you don't give up and as long as there is love, you hang in there, you fight for it, you remember the history, the good, the joy, the connection and you get through it. I wish I could have passed this on to Mark. Here I stand still trying to pick up the pieces. I don't want to fight with him and I'm not angry but I am damaged. I am still fighting to find any semblance of self-esteem and to find some kind of confidence in my appearance and desirability. I can't help but believe part of the reason he's not coming home is that what his mother said is true. He will find a reason to not come home, Mark doesn't like fat women. I no longer have the perfect body, I'm older now. I hope this isn't the case but I just feel that part of his decision is based on his desire for me physically is no longer there and that was a big part of us, the desire and lust we had for each other, without that I can't hold him.

I still have no security in my heart that he physically wanted me now I'm not thin or that I am still pretty or that my body is still ok for my age. It is those scars that I still carry every day that he can't see. It is those scars that still cause me to look at myself in the mirror each day and resent what I see and to feel so depressed that I can't turn back time. Some things I just can't change and one is that I can never turn back time, I can never be younger. I know he loved me but I also know that this is one element of a marriage and I also know that it is lust that gets you through the hard times. If in my heart I don't like what I see when I look at me and I don't feel desirable how do I get unbroken. I have lost part of me and I honestly at this point can't say that I will ever get that back. So throughout this book I have tried to give you the good and the bad. I have been completely honest with all the emotions that go along with being in love with a man that is unfaithful and also what happens when you hurt or are broken for whatever reason and turn to someone else that your choice may be the end of what you wanted so desperately to save. I have told you my deepest weaknesses and my most private thoughts. I hope you have gained some insight if you are going through this as I wish I had when I heard the news that someone else had stolen the lust of my husband and a part of his heart as well.

I don't know if there is an absolute answer to the question, once a cheater always a cheater, but I do know that it is a very personal journey to find out and the answer is not the same for each and every person. And be careful because I leaned what one is capable of maybe the other is as well and that is destined to destroy everything. My problem was I made the wrong choice and I lost the most important thing in my life. My husband, my lover, my best friend, my soul mate, the other half of me.

When I was younger and thought I knew absolutely everything there was to know about love, I used to talk with girlfriends and our take on the subject was always the same, if he cheated on me he'd be out the door.

How many of you used to have that exact thought yourselves?

One thing I have discovered thus far is that love is not black and white, love is very very complicated. I never knew how much a part of you another person could become until I was faced with losing the other half of me. I made the choice to try to forgive and to rebuild a strong marriage. My husband chose to walk away.

I'm not saying it is easy to stay because it is the farthest thing from that but I am saying that I believe that with hard work and a lot of self discovery, and if you are very very gentle with yourself and do things in your own time that it is possible to get there.

I believe that everyone makes mistakes and some are larger than others and take more time to get past but none of us are perfect. My how love would be easier if we were. I also believe that if someone loves you they won't hurt you on purpose and they will always put your heart above their own. It sometimes just takes some people longer to learn this than others. Some of us had great parents and were taught good lessons, which was the case with me yet still I made a mistake. Then there are others that didn't have it quite so good when they were younger, some that suffered abuse and neglect, which was the case for Mark. I understand this and I guess this is what enabled me to try and forgive and to continue to love. I understand that our childhoods build who we are, what our belief system will be and how we will handle ourselves in a relationship. I believe all of these factors need to be taken into consideration when you make the decision to stay or to go. I don't think Mark's infidelities were based solely on sexual gratification but were also based on a lack of self-worth that he held about himself.

As I said at the beginning of this book, I am not a professional but I am a woman and a wife. I know what I felt during this journey and I know also that I believed I would make it through with my marriage intact, I was wrong, maybe you will learn from my mistake and not add to the problem and maybe you will have a happy ending.

Remember as you take this journey, YOU ARE NOT ALONE!

Chapter Eighteen

Final Words

As I wrote this book, I had no other perspective but my own to give. I believe there are other women out there that have gone through as much as I have in the name of love and perhaps more, and it is for you that this book was written.

I wanted you to know that you're not alone and I hope hearing the story of my journey and understanding that if love is true, mistakes can be forgiven, will help you get through the troubled times. When you factor in the heartache that infidelity can cause not only to your marriage but to who you really are inside it is hugely important. But I guess what I am trying to convey is that when it comes to marriage I believe it is just as important to also factor in all the other parts that make a marriage a whole. It isn't just the physical that keeps a family together, there is so much more involved and it wasn't until twenty six years of loving this one person that I came to this realization. He was loving and accepting of my children and when push comes to shove he was almost always there when it counted.

I have written about the trials of infidelity in this book and portrayed my personal experiences as best I can, but I hope you can read between the lines. There was so much good and so many cherished memories between us that the bad and the mistakes weren't enough to end my love. If you have someone in your life that is the other half of you, I guess I just want you to see the big picture and take every part of your relationship into consideration before you make that final decision to stay or to go. Try to see where both of you came from what beliefs were instilled in you as a child. What does marriage and love and commitment mean to both of you because it doesn't always mean the same to everyone but that doesn't mean they aren't just as much in love, they just love differently. I don't know where I would be today had I just waited for him to help heal my broken self and not made the biggest mistake of my life out of loneliness, had I not been the one to hear all the false words from someone else at a very low point in my life, had I just waited for the man I love. I just know that there is something very deep inside of me that won't let him go and honestly I don't know if I ever can.

I hope in years to come I can look back on our relationship without the heartache and just treasure every memory I have. I don't regret my decision to stay, I really regret my decision to cheat, I regret hurting his heart, just because I had been hurt was no excuse, I was wrong. Don't make the same mistake I did if you still love your partner the way I do. I just love him. I prayed that someday I would hear the words come from him "I can finally say that I love you as much as you love me" and that I never again hear those words "I wish I loved you like you love me." I will never hear either. I lost the love of my life. If you are in this situation please think before you act, you might do something that you can't take back and lose the most important person in your life, I did. Find your own answers and follow your heart, there is a reason us women have intuition and if I can leave you with a word of advice I think it wold have to be, always trust your intuition for it is very seldom wrong.

Mark is the man I chose to give my heart to so many years ago and the man I still love today. He is the man that grew with me, that loved me in spite of himself, the man that took the journey with me and most of all, is the man that I will love for the rest of my life.